HOW A
WOODEN TERRACE
BECAME
AN ONLINE BUSINESS

ODD HELGE HVEDING

HOW A
WOODEN TERRACE
BECAME
AN ONLINE BUSINESS

Edited by Tim Challman

Oh2Musikk-Publishing

Published by Oh2Musikk AS
Norway

www.oh2musikk.com

Copyright 2017© by Odd Helge Hveding

Cover Artwork: Andrea White Hveding
Editing: TC Tolking

Manufactured in the United States of America
ISBN 978-82-691146-0-7

ACKNOWLEDGEMENTS

To be able to write this book, I owe a great thank you to all the marketers out there, who told me what to do through their work and sometimes their presence. I learned a lot of what works and what doesn't work, which showed me, why it was important to create this book as soon as possible. Thank you!

I would not be able to make this a reality without the great help and encouragement from my two fantastic coaches, Rainbow Abegg and Gregory Downey. Their inspirational teaching and their invaluable contribution in keeping myself on the edge through the whole process has improved every part of the book into the informational and educational book I wanted to create. Their insights, knowledge and warmhearted advice will forever stay as great examples in my life. Thank you!

The editor of the book, Tim Challman, accepted my wishes and patiently prepared the book into an understandable context, without letting go of my personal story. His great way of teaching how to improve the text on all levels needed, has been very satisfying, educational, challenging and fun at the same time. Thank you!

Last, but not least, my family needs to be thanked for all their contribution in keeping up the spirit, their help, advice, hints and support of the work through the whole process. An extra thanks to Andrea, my daughter, for the great job with the cover. I have a marvelous family and I am very grateful for each and every one, no exception. You all make my life perfect. Thank you!

Odd Helge Hveding

TABLE OF CONTENTS

ACKNOWLEDGEMENTS 5
FOREWORD – THEN CAME ODD 10

PREFACE..13
   IN THE BEGINNING THERE WAS A PROBLEM..........................18
   I WISH I KNEW THIS BEFORE I STARTED MY ONLINE CAREER...19
   THE JOURNEY TO SUCCESS..21
CHAPTER 1: ONLINE MARKETING - THE SIMPLE FACTS 28
   WHAT IS ONLINE MARKETING? 28
   THIS IS WHAT ONLINE MARKETERS REALLY DO 33
   THE EDUCATION YOU NEED...35
   ONLINE IS THE INTERNET 37
   MARKETING IS MARKETING 39
      Collect Information on a subject 42
      Express opinions...42
      Sell something 42
      Teach something 43
      How you can achieve success in 90 days? 44
   WHO ARE THE PEOPLE WHO SUCCEED FAST? 44
   HOW A WOODEN TERRACE BECAME AN ONLINE BUSINESS.....46
   Next Best Steps!..48
CHAPTER 2: THE POWER OF ONLINE MARKETING...............49
   WHY ONLINE MARKETING IS SO POWERFUL.......................49
   THE POWER INSIDE..52
   THE POWER OF THE TOOLS..53
   LEVERAGE 53
   WHAT YOU NEED TO SUCCEED – The Basic Marketing Tools.......57
      Website 57
      The costs 58
      Autoresponder 59
      Social media – What are they? 60
      What social media is good for online marketing? 61
      How to do social media marketing 63
      How to learn social media marketing 64
      Videos 65
      Communication tools..65
      App – Short for application................................66
   THE SKILLS YOU NEED TO SUCCEED....................................66

Practice your communication..66
Practice your ability to type...67
Never underestimate the power of shortcuts..........................67
The basics of the tools..68
THE KNOWLEDGE YOU WANT TO HAVE...68
YOUR MINDSET IS YOUR POWER 70
THE RESCUE HABITS AND TOOLS..72
HOW TO MAKE DOLLARS WANT YOU ONLINE......................................73
YOU CAN DO ALL OF THIS - IT AWAITS YOUR ACTIONS 76
Next Best Steps!...77
CHAPTER 3: HOW TO TURN YOUR PASSION INTO PROFIT..........................79
WHAT IS PASSION AND HOW TO FIND YOURS 81
START YOUR PASSIONATE SEARCH FOR YOUR PASSION - NOW
....84
WHAT YOU ARE LOOKING FOR WITHOUT KNOWING IT.............................85
THE CAVEMAN METHOD..85
Introduction 86
Focus on the outcome 87
Your imagination 90
DOLLARS WANT YOU..94
MONEY – THE GOOD AND BAD 96
BE AWARE OF WHAT YOU DON'T WANT YOUR MONEY TO DO
....98
BE AWARE OF WHAT YOU WANT YOUR MONEY TO DO.............................102
NOTHING CAN STOP YOU, UNLESS YOU LET IT...............................104
WHAT DO THINGS LOOK LIKE WHEN YOU LET DOLLARS WANT
YOU? 106
WHEN YOU'RE GRATEFUL AND SHOW IT, THIS HAPPENS........................108
Next Best Steps!...109
CHAPTER 4: HOW TO MASTER A PROGRESSIVE SKILL SET 110
YOU HAVE AN IDEA...115
MAKE THE IDEA SIMPLE 116
MULTIPLYING THE IDEA 119
WHO WANTS THIS?..119
MAKE YOUR PLAN...120
YOUR MARKETING PLAN – THE STEPS YOU TAKE...............................121
EFFINCIENCY OF SIMPLICITY 122
THE PEOPLE 123
WHERE AND WHEN YOU ADVERTISE MATTERS..................................124
YOUR TIME – YOUR RESPONSIBILITY.......................................128
YOUR PROGRESS DEPENDS ON YOUR SKILLS 131
6 STEPS ON YOUR WAY TO SUCCESS 133

Next Best Steps!.. 135
CHAPTER 5: HOW TO OVERCOME OBSTACLES THAT PREVENT
SUCCESS 136
   THE TIME YOU HAVE 137
   YOUR NUMBER ONE ASSET 141
   WHEN TO WORK? 146
   WHEN TO HAVE FUN? 148
   SLEEP AND HOW IT MAKES YOU BETTER 150
   TAKE CONTROL AND MAKE YOUR LIFE 152
   PRACTICE USING YOUR TIME WISELY 153
   THE TECHNOLOGICAL OBSTACLES 155
      Your knowledge about the tools 155
   RUN YOUR BUSINESS WHILE YOU DEVELOP YOUR SKILLS 159
   SOCIAL CONNECTIONS AND THE PRACTICAL CONSEQUENCES
   160
   PROCRASTINATIONS 161
   THERE IS ALWAYS A SOLUTION 165
   CELEBRATE 166
   Next Best Steps! 167
CHAPTER 6: DEVELOP A WINNING MINDSET 169
   THE HUNT 174
   BE AWARE OF WHAT YOU DON'T WANT 178
   BE AWARE OF WHAT YOU WANT 184
   BEWARE OF WHAT IS STOPPING YOU – THE LIMITING BELIEFS
   187
   LIMITING BELIEFS 188
   HOW TO BE RID OF THE LIMITING BELIEFS 192
   VISUALIZE YOUR GOALS 193
   SURRENDER 195
   Next Best Steps! 196
CHAPTER 7: HOW TO PRODUCE CONSISTENT RESULTS 198
   CONSISTENCY 198
   BAD HABITS – THE HABITS NOT SERVING YOU 201
   GOOD HABITS – THE HABITS SERVING YOU 204
   HOW TO CHANGE A HABIT TO SERVING YOU 205
   PAY ATTENTION TO THE NEW HABITS 206
   SERVICE YOUR NEW HABITS 207
   CONSISTENT RESULTS – HOW TO PRODUCE THEM 208
   MARKETING AUTOMATION? 209
   BUILDING YOUR LIST 211
   WHEN YOU ACHIEVE YOUR GOALS 212
   Next Best Steps! 216

CHAPTER 8: DESIGN THE LIFE YOU TRULY DESERVE 217

BEING NEW IS BEING NEW 222

SOLUTION NUMBER ONE – EVERYONE DOES THIS 225

SOLUTION NUMBER TWO – YOU CAN'T NOT DO IT 226

CAREER CHANGE OR A JOB CHANGE? 229

WHAT IS A CAREER CHANGE? 229

WHAT STUFF ARE YOU MADE OF? 230

DO YOU KNOW WHAT YOU WANT TO DO? 231

THE DIFFERENCE: WANT TO DO – DOING IT 232

WANT TO WORK AT HOME? 234

BUSINESS ONLINE 235

There are platforms and there are systems 235

Different platforms 236

BUSINESS – sounds worse than it is 238

THE TRAINING YOU NEED 238

DESIGN THE LIFE YOU TRULY DESERVE 239

NOW IS ALWAYS A GOOD TIME TO SURRENDER 242

Next Best Steps! 245

FOREWORD – Then Came Odd

I've been involved in personal coaching in one capacity or another since January of 2005. I've coached several millionaires, a couple of billionaires, people of average or above average income, and even some that were so broke that they probably had no business enrolling in coaching to begin with. That's not to say that coaching wasn't good for them. Because, regardless of financial status, nearly every coaching client of mine has gone on to achieve more with coaching than they would have without. But never in all of my years as an executive-mindset, leadership, and authorship coach have I worked with a person that I could honestly say, "This person probably would have changed the entire course of their life with or without the help of a coach"; then came Odd.

Perhaps he wouldn't have made as much progress in as little time. But, the truth is he was bound and determined to make some major life changes and to share those changes with others.

There is something that has to be said about a guy that is generally positive and cheerful in spite of living in a region of the globe that is blistering cold and completely dark for the nearly half of the year. In fact, he's one of the most pleasant people I have ever come to know not just as a client but also as a friend.

Odd Hveding came into my coaching calendar with a single desire at heart: to share a message that would help other people to have a better life. More specifically, he wants to help people to have a more prosperous and abundant life: a life that is constrained neither by time nor money.

Over the years and through a great deal of trial and error, he has become quite convinced (and for very good reason) that anyone anywhere with enough desire and determination to learn and a decent internet connection can become free from the grind of daily labor through e-commerce. I believe him whole-heartedly and so should you. Not just because I say you should believe him. But, because everything that is shared in this book is exactly what I wish I had learned BEFORE I ever began my journey into online business education - *and then some.* And I do mean - *and then some.* But best of all, if you're just naive enough to do exactly what he asks you to do along the way, without question, the results that you will get will speak volumes louder than the praises that I can sing about the contents of this book.

I have witnessed the creation of this masterpiece. I have not just read it, but I have read it aloud to the author so that he could hear the power and genius of his own creation.

May the power and genius of this wonderful literary creation allow you to not to just make a living but to Design the Life That You Truly Deserve.

Happy Living,

Gregory Downey

Author of Attracting Miracles (And My Secret Life as a Miracles Coach)

PREFACE

"How a Wooden Terrace Became an Online Business", is my map to the lifestyle I want to live instead of just making a living. My trombone, my beloved brother, is my driver. It is music that inspires me and my why for creating a steady income. Let me explain. I realized that I need money and a stream of income but perhaps not a job. This new reality totally rocked my world. Could I give up my teaching job? How would I survive? I turned to the world wide web! There is money out there to attract! I could tap into that endless funding power and release myself from the worker bee mentality. You know, where you get up in the morning, concerned with how this day will turn out, getting myself to work and do what I'm supposed to do. When you have done that for some time, there is a chance that you will get the feeling of being in the wrong place. It doesn't have to be because it is a bad place to be, at least it wasn't for me; it's the feeling of being in the position of moving on, doing something else for the good of some other people or doing something differently when I wanted to, not when I had a chance to do it. The worker bees get to work just a few days after they are born. Their first job is to clean out their own birthplace. Then they change to another job inside the beehive, taking care of everything inside, and in the last phase of their life they get outside to collect pollen for making honey. They do that until they are totally worn out. They simply die of exhaustion, and that's it.

I stumbled upon an article about the bee hive, I got fascinated by the fact that there are so many similarities with how we humans live our lives. I had to read some more about it, and the more I read, the more it reminded me of the way my life had started to become. It was as if there was no way out. Every opening for adjustments or trying something new seemed to be closed. I felt caged. You know the feeling of always being on the move for something, but constantly longing to do something else, having the feeling that something else would be much more important than what you actually do. It's a longing for the moment when you can relax and enjoy life, instead of an urgent need to go to bed, because you have to get ready for the next day, doing something other than what you really want to do. That is where I was. I just had to do something to get rid of the repetition of it all, the lack of excitement, never having the time to sit down and spend time on what my life was about. Every bee has its function; in many ways, so do we, but I got the sense of being wanted elsewhere, and that is what I started to look for. I had no idea what would come of it, but I started to do something, and what I have experienced along the way is a fairytale worth living. A few hints about where to begin occurred to me, and they were based on what I had tried to realize earlier in life. Music has always been there, more or less, so maybe I wasn't so far away. I decided to give it a shot. I wanted to record my music.

After all, there are millions of people who have never heard my music and I had loved music since I was a child. I even wrote some pieces as a child, not that you need to listen to them, but it's a good laugh for me.

It all started with the Beatles. I heard a song by them on the radio and I was hooked. I remember my first introduction to my future. The trombone. I just had to play it, so I bought one. It was the first time I listened to my own internal moorings.

Trombone player

It is such a wonderful and fascinating instrument, a survivor of the Renaissance. You see, it's the feeling. When you look at it, the glint of the shiny metal is captivating and when I pick up the trombone I fall in love. The slide has been lubricated lovingly and moves with ease, it makes the feeling so delicate, it makes me want to play. There is no resistance when I move the slide gently in and out. When my lips touch the mouthpiece and I blow air through it, the sound of the Gods come "alive". It is magical and it is my reason for online marketing.

I learned music as a 10-year-old boy and I grew into a skilled musician who was one with my instrument, and then I became a teacher. I feel I am most myself when I create music, by playing, teaching or composing. It is the harmony of my life. It is my masterpiece and passionate state of mind. This is my state of perfection and it has taken practice to get there. Yes, for me music is life. It is my lifestyle and I am curious how I ended up in a beehive because I am actually a musician. Well, I've been lucky to have always worked with music in the schools, but still... I was drafted into the education system and found myself lost in this maze. I have loved the teaching, but the hive – not so much.

I had to go deep inside myself to find the right questions, like "How do we get out of the hive and into a life style?" There is money to be made because bills have to be paid, but I started to believe that getting out of the hive and into the music of life was the answer. I found something about online marketing and found a possible solution. Online marketing is the way to the field of infinite possibilities. This is an easy map to online marketing containing a lot of space and infinite possibilities.

Where to begin....

Remember:
You don't want a living, you want a lifestyle.

I was reading an e-book. It was about how to write your success story. I read this sentence: "You can't sit on the sidelines and expect everything to fall in place."

Well, I was sitting, but I didn't expect everything to fall in place. I understood it was time to take action. So I did.

Success is a word we normally use for people who make it big time. They must be very lucky people. Well, the lucky people, winning millions in a lottery, usually end up with a debt they can't repay. Successful people are different. They all have a few traits in common. Success is taking action, step by step and develop habits the right way. I'm here to show you the basic steps to help you get started. One step at a time. You are designed for success and in this book, you will find how I showed up for me.

Success, by the way, is a part of your daily life. It is there, but you may not allow yourself to call it a success. There are areas of your life in which you are successful, but maybe you are so used to these that you don't notice them anymore. Other areas of life have been successful, but you don't do them any-more. It is up to you to decide what success is. For some people, it's all about money; for others it's all about what money can get you, and for still others, it's all about what you can do in your life, and nothing else matters. There are also those who turn their hobbies into a lifestyle with success. Others care about who they are for others and how they do that successfully. I want to challenge you in this book, to make you see how successful your life can be and how online marketing can make your life even more successful. In the beginning, everything looks ordinary, but as you get better you scale it up, naturally and life starts changing for the better and better and better.

Let's start by learning a wonderful word that can change everything: Yet.

When you say, "I'm not a success", please allow yourself to end that sentence with the word Yet.

Here we go:
"I'm not a success, yet."

You can be a success, because you are a success. Just the fact that YOU ARE, is a success. You made it, so far.
Now just a few adjustments are needed here and there, and You Will Become A Great Success.

You'll understand the power of the word "yet", and how it can change things for you as you read on. It has changed a lot for me and others and is partially why I wrote this book. I suggest you let me tell you why I wrote this book and what you can expect to find inside here.

IN THE BEGINNING
THERE WAS A PROBLEM

I was sitting outside my house. I had just finished building a wooden terrace. It was a solution that made my gardening a lot easier, so I made the drawing, planned it, bought the materials and constructed it. It was such a great feeling to finish it. When you do that kind of work, you do some thinking, and during the three weeks I spent on this, one thought recurred: I want to record my music. More for the process than the popularity. Having my own music recorded means more to me than being popular.

The recording process is easy, but it has to be done, and it does cost money. Since I'd never cared especially about money, I had to find a way to earn more, so that I could afford the recording process. It didn't have to be the most expensive kind of recording, but a recording I could be proud of. Since the music was recorded, I decided I could just as easily go for an international release.

Sitting on my own handmade terrace, I just decided to make sure this happened. Whatever the cost, I wanted my music recorded and I knew what tracks I wanted on it, and I had to have a concert on the release date. I got this image of how the cover of the CD would look. The title was chosen quickly and I was just about to release it, when it hit me... Stop dreaming. Do it!

Let's first record the music, make the cover, make sure all the rights are properly reserved and pay all the people involved. I could have done all that really quickly, except for the money part. I never learned anything about money. It was time to check the Internet on how to make money.

Online marketing, here we go!

I WISH I KNEW THIS BEFORE I STARTED MY ONLINE CAREER

Full of enthusiasm I started my computer, browsing for how to make money online. I was overwhelmed by the fact that there were close to 300 million sites telling me how to do this. It had to be possible.

After a day or two (I honestly don't remember), I started to get the hang of it, the search, I mean. The different approaches to making money online started to make a pattern. Some sites were almost scary, they had a scent of something I didn't want to touch, while others seemed more friendly and not so full of the hype way of presenting it.

I ended on a site with a program. They actually had a system that would make me money within 90 days. Great! This was so easy, and I entered the program, completed the setup they told me to do and started the training. I was lucky. I had found a way to make money online, and in only 90 days or less!

Consistency was a very big part of this. I had to do some tasks daily and when I did, I would succeed. Nice! I did my best, but as I went along, new tasks were added, all the time I had available was spent learning something new, and then something else and new skills I had to learn continued to appear. Some of these skills were quite difficult for me. I had never done anything like it, so it did take some time. I learned something new every day, did my daily tasks and listened carefully to what they told me to do. Every day there was yet another new thing I had to learn. After two weeks, I was trying to learn so many things at the same time that I really got confused. Instead of managing consistent work, it became consistent confusion. I lost track of where I was. I had problems completing the daily tasks due to lack of time and I didn't actually learn anything. Everything got mixed together, and I was completely lost. I didn't stop, still believing that this had to be the way things had to be done. Every week a webinar where everyone was talking about how much they had struggled and how lucky I was to have this program that had everything all laid out for me.

Ninety days later, I had managed to build something. I wasn't proud of it, but I had something to improve. That's a normal feeling, I was told, and since other people knew, I had to believe them. I'd had one sale and was thrilled about that, but what about the rest? I had done everything they told me, but I wasn't exactly making money. I was paying money. There's nothing wrong with paying money, but when you expect to make more than you pay, something is wrong.

That's when I started to really understand why 98 percent of people starting marketing online fail. I didn't have all the answers, but I had an idea of what could go wrong, why it usually did and why just a few achieved the success we all wanted.

I made a decision that in my business, this should not happen that easily. I left that program, carried out new searches, found more ways to get rid of my money on Internet. I kept the needed information about the different ways of doing online marketing, the good things and the bad things. I also started to look for a combination of the good things out there, how to put it together to really help people get a good start with online marketing. My lack of success would not be in vain. I wanted to help people avoid the traps and build their success in 90 days. Thousands of people have made it, so it is possible.

This book tells you what you need to know before you start your online career.

THE JOURNEY TO SUCCESS

This is not a book about my success. This is a book about my journey to success. I have read tons of books about successful people – what they did, how they got there and what living a wealthy life feels like (which was their goal). It's easy and enjoyable reading, a lot clumsier to get there, but fun when you know how you can get there. It's also a lot easier to laugh at all the mistakes, misunderstandings and other flaws you meet along the way. Success is the journey to get there, to reach your goals and achieve the lifestyle you want because of what you did.

Successful people have a lot in common. You can and should read all about that in all the books (don't worry, you will find a lot of the common ideas here as well), but there are a lot of facts they never tell you. There are some actions you have to take to make yourself successful. Writers usually don't tell you this in their books because they have implemented some of these actions and skills so deeply themselves that they forget their importance or don't consider them a part of the challenges you are facing. You want to be at the point when you are building your platform to make your online marketing a success.

I was physically sitting on my personal platform, when I had that great idea, and I had built it myself. I, (like in me), had done something, and it was a success, so it was time to move on. I just call it a hint about what to do, how to do it and (very important) the fact that now is always a good time to start taking action.

It is easy to succeed if you are prepared for your success. The preparation is probably different from what you expect it to be. If you know what you want, you develop the desire to know how to get there, without a map. The more you know, the wider your horizon, the faster you will find your path to the platform where you can build your lifestyle.

You see, you are already a success. Your uniqueness is greater than most people know. You have successfully become who you are. No one else. The chance of being you is actually very small. You are one of more than eight million options among the cells of which two united the day you were conceived. Those two cells won a contest involving about 40–600 million competitors. That's what I call a real victory. What you see when you look in the mirror is the person you have successfully become, because you did what you did, since the day you were born.

- You were prepared for being born and you made it. Success!
- You grew up, learned a lot, among other things, how to eat by yourself. Success!
- You are what you are as a result of all the things you have done. Since no one else has done all the things you have done, and the fact that you have done them differently than anyone else, you have strengthened your own uniqueness. Success!

You have talents. Everybody has talents, but we don't always know what our talents are. If you haven't found your talent, you have something great to look forward to. Your talents may even be there already, without you knowing it, because you don't see it as a talent.

I have had my successes in areas of my life. I'm grateful for all the help I have received from a lot of my friends and friendly people who have helped me to succeed. I am certain that you have experienced the same.

What is your talent?
What is your passion?

There are periods of my life when I have been work-ing days and nights to learn some new skills and follow where my curiosity led me. Some of these periods have been very exhausting, but others have been very exciting. Before I needed money, I was never interested in money, so I had to change that. I've always known that my basic need for money will be covered, and it has always been covered. I came to a point where I needed more money to make my dreams come true, so I had to learn how to desire money, instead of needing it. This has been a very exciting journey; I've learned a lot and I can use it.

Life is about learning something new that makes your coming days better and more exciting.

The experience of doing something you're not good at, is in fact learning a lot about yourself. At times, you don't know where to go next, because life took a different direction than you expected. After a while, you start expecting the unexpected, which is great.

When you begin on a new path in life, you have a great feeling of this being right. There is of course this feeling of nervousness, but it is not nervous-ness, it is you being on the alert for what will come next. You have experienced them, but lately society has made those moments more and more in-frequent, so in some cases this feeling and aware-ness is misunderstood as anxiety. People think they are afraid of the situation they're in. They are not used to being exposed to something completely new. They believe it must be dangerous, and danger makes us either crawl into ourselves or run for our lives. We want to hide from any kind of danger, and this is one of the main reasons people keep their life as it is, not because they like it, but they know what it is like. Don't get me wrong, anxiety exists, and people being anxious should get help from professionals, but the anxiety I am talking about is similar to that feeling of uncertainty and being uncomfortable when you are about to take the big step into something you never did before.

I've had to overcome many situations when I didn't feel comfortable. I noticed how this feeling was very close to the feeling of being anxious. When you are in a more or less anxious state of mind, you might tremble, you listen very closely to every sound, and you hear many sounds you didn't know existed. This feeling is very similar to what you feel when you are about to go on stage. As a musician, I've taken the stage many times. You get used to it, but when the entire setting is new, you are not used to it. You are what we call nervous, but well prepared. Your preparation makes you get through this experience, and you feel great at the other end.

My first exam as a trombone player was probably an ok concert. I don't know, I don't remember. Over the years, a few snapshots here and there have showed up. They can easily be something I believe I have experienced, but it can also be me internalizing what people who were there have told me. In general, I only remember playing the three or four first notes, and the applause after 45 minutes. They told me it sounded good; I just had to take their word for it. I was well prepared for the concert (the exam was a 45-minute long concert), and I had practiced all the drills and the repertoire was picked by me; I had found a sequence in which to play the pieces that made it possible to play for 45 minutes. I had also practiced being nervous. I made some exercises and practiced while doing them. It probably helped me, I don't know, I wasn't there - despite the fact that an audience was present and they actually saw me on stage.

The next concert in which I was playing solo was some months later. I lifted my trombone, inhaled and started to play. I let the instrument tell the story while I kept enjoying the great feeling of moving the slide and changing the pitch accurately, with all the love I had. It sounded good and it felt wonderful. Great applause came afterwards, and I was present the whole time. That was a great experience. I would probably not have had this particular experience, if it wasn't for my "mysterious" exam.

The journey to success will always be full of surprising moments. If you knew everything that was going to happen and what to do, you would have done it a long time ago. It is all about keeping going, and it is about believing in yourself. Life is a series of challenges, and what you have learned from all those challenges is knowledge that makes you stronger. You will find a stronger self and a wonderful personality underneath, even more wonderful than you are today.

If I had played my exam today, I would have taken a completely different approach. I wouldn't have been nervous; I would have played the concert, had fun, remembered everything and laughed if something went wrong.

Now I know what I should have known that day. Now I understand why this happens. Now I know what to do to get on top of the situation, and that knowledge is worth more than anything. I wouldn't know this if I hadn't had these experiences, so I'm grateful for all the experiences that got me to the point where I am now. And now. And now. And...

As you read on, I will give you examples of why that actually will make you a better self, if you allow it, that is.

Your uniqueness, your skills, your knowledge, your passion and talents are all part of what makes you a success. When you know what feeling you are looking for and let it go, you will be amazed when you experience its constant presence.

Online marketing is a growing way of making an income or just some extra money or just a lot of fun. This book is about how you can make your success richer, more nuanced and, if you look closely, you can distinguish between being selfish and being a better self. You want to know that too.

For many people, this starts with understanding the power of Yet.

... and by the way, I am recording my music now.

Chapter 1

ONLINE MARKETING - THE SIMPLE FACTS

WHAT IS ONLINE MARKETING?

Some years ago, I was in the lucky state of becoming a father, for the third time. There was one problem, though; our house was too small...

We needed a bigger house, but our financial situation didn't exactly support the idea. Just recovering from a huge debt, everything concerning money was creating stress and a sense of anxiety. Still, we had to go through with it and we were looking at a lot of houses, searching for one that served the purpose of having enough space, being within a decent price range and being in an area that made it practical to get to work and our other obligations.

First we had to sell the small house we had. I was quite frustrated and I kept talking about it all day, among friends, at work and everywhere I was. I got a suggestion for the price of the house and was about to start advertising in the local newspaper. I decided that would do. When I was working on how to formulate the advertisement, the phone rang. This was a person who had heard that I was going to sell the house. I was a bit amazed; after all, I hadn't started to promote it yet. We finished the conversation and made a deal that I would call back when I was ready with the paperwork. I continued working on this announcement, but I got another call, within the same hour from someone else who also wanted to buy the house. Weird, was my thought, but again, if two persons wanted to buy the house, let's let one of them have it. I never got to the marketing of the house in the paper. It was sold a week later, for a price I wouldn't dare to ask when we started. It was also enough to get the financial situation in good shape for buying a house big enough for the expanding family. This was a successful moment of marketing, I just didn't know it at the time.

Rumors will have it that online marketing is the best way to lose money. It can be, but it doesn't have to be. When you know the simple facts about online marketing, you understand how you can deal with it; you will know more about what you are looking for and at the end of the chapter, I've entered the steps you should take to start your journey in a way that makes it fun, keeps it easy and hopefully helps you avoid getting lost in the jungle of opportunities.

When you have finished this chapter, you will *begin to* understand how simple it really is, and *you will* probably get an idea of how you can design your own online marketing. You will also start to understand how to look beyond the obstacles and focus on what matters, the efficiency of simplicity.

When I started my marketing, I didn't know anything about why one did this or that. I was told to do it, and I did. My results were really bad, for a long time. My "system" became a really chaotic bunch of electronic documents, papers, recordings, and it broke down completely. There was just one thing to do, namely start over and try to make a better system, which, of course broke down as I went along in the process. Whatever time I had available went toward making the system better and better. I got addicted, kept on improving, learning more, testing more, trying out more, always with the conviction that this time it would work. I simply knew I would get a lot of customers.

The truth is, no one was interested in what I had to offer. At least that was my excuse, based on the rationale that a lot of others made it work, doing the same thing as I did. Why didn't people like my marketing?

I got used to keep doing what I should do without any customers turning up. I still believed that my "system" had to be right and the customers would come. Every time I tested something new, convinced that it would result in vast numbers of customers, nothing happened...

Then one day...

A customer! What do I do now???

I had been told that customers would follow the system I had set up, but nobody told me I had to speak to my customers. (*Can you feel the panic?*) In that particular system, talking to the customers was very important to make them buy the products. Communication had never been a problem for me, until then. I didn't know what to say, I didn't know what to do. I felt sorry for my customer, because I didn't have a clue about what to do. I realized I had to learn how to speak to my customers. My brain was screaming: "How do we speak to customers?"

I found a solution, and it worked, partly, at least. There are many ways of speaking to a customer. The first rule is letting them know who you are and why they want to buy the product or service you offer, you are a lot closer than I was. I was good at making systems that didn't work, or was it something else? All kinds of doubts started to turn up, out of the blue. It got really hard to do the daily tasks, I was not convinced it would work.

I believed that communication online was a different way of communicating. It isn't, communication is communication. The only difference is that you can communicate with people from the whole world. You can communicate through all the channels you normally use to communicate with people, talk to them, use a phone, any kind of video chatting, social media or through e-mail. I knew about all of these but not how to use them as a part of my marketing.

My search for answers gave a lot of results, or to be honest – just one. There's one thing that successful people have in common, no matter what kind of success they have. It's more important than communication; it is the basic of the basics:

You have to be yourself and do what you love.

This is the essential part of a successful marketing campaign. When you are yourself and you love to do what you do, you will communicate with your customers or visitors naturally. You talk about what you have in common, you talk about what you are marketing and you talk about it because you love it.

Do what you love, and make sure it is what you love. Don't enter a program because someone tells you that you can get $3000 dollars a month in 90 days. You may feel you want that, but that is not what you want.

You are looking for the reason behind your desire for money, or the reason behind the desire for marketing online. 98% of beginner marketers fail within the first year. Becoming part of programs that work perfectly for those who love to do what the programs offer, succeed. Most people don't succeed because we all have our particular talents, interests, passions and dreams. The 98% don't know this. They are new to using online marketing as a tool for making their success a reality. You cannot build your success on other people's dreams.

There are also a couple of other things you would like to know and I will tell you more in the next chapter of this book. For your information, it is possible to make $3000 dollars a month in 90 days, when you are ready to do so. You are ready when you know what You want to do and how to do it.

THIS IS WHAT ONLINE MARKETERS REALLY DO:

There are mainly two things you do when you begin online marketing:

1. you attract people
2. you attract money

It's not very probable that you would attract anything else. (You have to let me know immediately if you find something else). You don't have to make money to be a success online, but you can choose to make money. If you just want to attract people, you use the same principles for marketing as when you attract money. Sounds weird? Well, it is a kind of weird, but not when you understand the meaning of attraction.

Let's imagine you have this huge interest in health improvement. When you have an interest, you tend to speak about it often. People get to know you as one who has a lot of knowledge about health improvement and maybe takes a particular action to improve your health. You are known for it within a certain circle of people. When your way of expressing yourself makes it so interesting that people come asking for advice or want you to answer their questions, you are a kind of a magnet. Magnets have a tendency of attracting or repelling, so if you don't attract, you repel. This is what happens in online marketing as well, it's like this:

1. Either you attract people or you repel people.
2. Either you attract money or you repel money.

This is the first important principle of all kind of marketing, not only online marketing, but any kind of marketing. People like what you present or they don't. There will always be both. Your goal is to attract the people who like what you are doing and let the others live their lives their way. If you make your marketing an attraction, some of the people who weren't looking for what you offer may recommend it to other people; that is a bonus.

You may have heard someone say "it's simple, it's just not easy." This is sometimes true, but if you are a person who easily gets in touch with other people, it can also be easy. If you have a passion or talent for what you are doing, this will shine through your marketing. If you have a problem getting to know people, you can still make your marketing a success; your passion will guide you. What you are marketing, what experience you have in the use of the Internet and the time you have available to do the proper workload matters only for the question of when you will succeed, but if you do what you love, you will succeed.

You are very special, but at the same time you are not so different from other people. As people, we have a lot in common and if other people can make this a reality, you can make it a reality, as soon as you are ready to start your success story. Then you can write a book on your journey and help other people to succeed with their marketing campaigns (just a suggestion).

You can get the simple things into an easy rolling money magnet, making you an income you wouldn't believe unless you saw it. If you're not looking for money, only people, you would attract more and more of them as well.

Let's get one thing straight:
Money can't talk or move.

Money needs people to take the action needed to make money.

This is the main reason why you should not focus on money. You should make sure that it is the money that wants you, through the people who can make money move.

As you can see, whether you want money or not, focusing on the people is what causes the success. When you get success, you recognize it and an ocean of possibilities opens to you.

THE EDUCATION YOU NEED

You can find some evening classes on how to get your business up and running. The problem with these is finding the time to get all the work done that you need to do between classes. What is good about them is that you meet people who are in the same situation as you. They want to build a business online, and you can discuss the subject with these people.

There are also online courses. They enable you to learn when it suits you. By scheduling when to move on and keeping to the schedule, you will be able to achieve the necessary combination of developing your business and grow along with it. You may find a course where you get the help you need, or a forum where you can search for the answers you need or by getting in touch with people who have the answers. More and more courses add this function to their program.

You will probably not find everything they should have told you, though. None of the courses I have taken told me everything. They always leave something out, not necessarily because they wanted to leave it out, but very often because they keep it on a need to know basis. Sometimes that is a good idea, but not always. You want to make sure that what you want to do online is covered in the training you receive.

When you are completely new to online marketing, you probably don't know so much about building websites. You need to learn that; it is easy, but a bit strange if you haven't done it before. The best way to start is to have a dedicated purpose for making the site. It makes it a lot easier; you have a completely different motivation to make it happen.

Another important area you want to learn more about is how you advertise on the Internet. There are many ways to do this; it's not difficult (and it doesn't have to be expensive), but you need to know something about it. You should also learn how to use your social media in a way that benefits your business. Many customers find their way to new online stores through social media. It is about being where the people are. The better your skills are, the better your marketing will be.

The third important area that can be of great help for your online marketing, is the use of email. Emails are still important in online marketing and are used by most of the successful online marketers to keep in touch with their customers.

This book will tell you more about all these three areas of online marketing, because they are basic. Some will say that you only need a website, and they are right, but they usually leave out that it may take a long time before you see the customers. The combinations of website (or websites), social media and the use of email is a faster way of getting customers to your online business, at least for the majority of marketers. You do want your success faster, right?

First let's have a look at what we are talking about.

ONLINE IS THE INTERNET

I didn't have a clue about anything when I started. I was a well qualified user of the Internet, but never gave it a thought to check what it really was. I had made some websites, just for fun. I had to program the first one myself. I don't remember anything from it, I'm just happy I don't have to do it anymore. Programming is fun for those who like it, but if you don't, there is a big chance that you'll never understand it. I wouldn't worry about that, because most website providers have more or less made the site for you. All you have to do is fill in the blanks. There is a bit more, but you don't need an education to understand it anymore. If you have training, that's great, but if you don't, you are probably among the majority of marketers out there. Use the Internet for what it's worth. When you wonder about something, search for it on the Internet. Someone has made the video or written the article that you need. The answers to all your questions are probably out there. Learning how to search, is a smart move. This is the way you can learn a lot more than you thought you were capable of, and suddenly, you are the expert.

The moment I started I was thrilled by how easy it was, the first week... They told me what to do and told me to keep doing it every day. It shouldn't take too much time. Not knowing what "too much time" meant, made it quite complicated. It didn't have to be complicated, but I made it complicated. Trying to be the best, I just kept on working on my website and my marketing campaign, without ever feeling I got anywhere. I didn't know what I should focus on, so I just tried to make something that looked good. After a period in this chaotic situation, I started to understand the importance of two things. I made myself a library of the routines I used, and I started to make notes of what to do and what I had been doing, more or less a diary. A pattern appeared, and when I understood the point of working in patterns, or habitual routines, things started to move a lot faster. My memory got a boost as well, I didn't have to look everything up from my library all the time. It became fun again. I started to have a great time, still learning something new every day, but also spending less time on each task. I could sit down, do what I was supposed to do, and then I could close the laptop, knowing I was on my way to success.

Internet is only a bunch of websites put together by millions of people (and growing). The websites may not look like they are websites, but that is all they are, they just look different from each other due to the programming behind what you see.

The Internet is an international connection, telephone lines coupled up to work very fast, so you can get all the information you want, find all the meanings of every word, who is who and what is what. You can buy everything you want and you can get all the training you want. If you are lonely, you can end that by joining the social media of your choice and meet people to chat with, talk to, share live video screening and even work on the same documents together.

All of those actions are presented on a website. Their appearance makes them look very different from each other. This only shows that the possibilities are enormous. The only thing that stops you from getting what you want from the Internet, is you. It doesn't have to be that way; you can change it into whatever you want it to be. You may have an idea of what you want, but if you don't have one, you hopefully will when you've finished this chapter, at least you will know your first goal: find your reason why.

Many beginner marketers are afraid that what you want to market is already massively exposed. They are not wrong, but they forget their own uniqueness. The way you will tell your story, or the way you will run your business, is different from everyone else, because there is only one of you. You attract other people than your competitors do, and of course, it's also the other way around. Your competitors attract other people than you do, whether you are attracted to what they do or not.

MARKETING IS MARKETING

Have you been to any kind of store lately? We all need food, for instance, so most of us frequent a store selling food of some kind. They have a product that you want, your kind of food, so you go into the shop, buy what you intended to buy and then leave happily, if you appreciate what you found.

If you didn't find what you were looking for, you're not quite as happy because you have to visit another store. If you asked for that specific product, and the staff member told you where you could get that product, you will return to that store later. They provided the service you needed to get what you wanted. When you have found what you were looking for, you know what store to visit for that product, but you also remember the other store, with the kind staff. You will probably visit both stores again, for different reasons. You have learned something, and this knowledge will return to you as soon as you need it again.

I got this customer one day. A nice guy, but he wasn't quite sure whether to join my business or not. We had a few conversations over a couple of weeks, I didn't want to push him, but scheduled a new call every time. After a few weeks, he seemed very stressed about the whole situation, so I asked him about the problem. He told me there was another marketer who was too eager to sell him a lot of stuff and never left him in peace. He made a decision there and then; he ended up buying my product. Partly so he could tell the other marketer that he wasn't interested, but also because he felt more comfortable with my offer. There were others taking the other offer, some of them because they felt they had to, but others because they liked the other marketing style better. It's just like music. Some people like my kind of music, while others have different preferences. My customers like my style, while others don't. That is a part of being in a market. You can't please everyone, but the more choices available, the more customers find what they are looking for on your website.

The way you will do your marketing, makes your business attractive for the people who have the same interests as you (with the possible exceptions of all the reasons in the world or just some...). Anyway, One of your goals should be to make every visitor a returning visitor. If you keep developing your websites, your skills and knowledge, you will be better at changing your sites, the articles and your product presentations all the time. Spending some time every now and then to improve what you have published online, makes your business more and more interesting for more and more people. When you have found your first customer, and earned your first dollar, you should start developing that way of marketing. Customers are people, and if one is interested, there will always be more people interested.

This is marketing. When you know where to find what you're looking for, the store has run a great marketing campaign and is rewarded with customers coming to buy what they sell. Competition can't be avoided, but when you are good at giving service, people will remember your store for more than your products. That is an advantage. Be nice to people and you are rewarded with more customers. This is essential for your marketing and gives you a great online reputation, so to speak. You want that, and you'll notice you are welcome.

Marketing can be about a lot of things. You don't always have to communicate directly with the people, other than what you display on your site. This depends on what you are marketing. The next chapter goes deeper into the marketing, what you need, where to find it and how powerful online marketing can be. In this chapter, we are looking at the basic of the basics, without any disturbing offers. When you see how simple it really is, you will begin to understand how you can make anything online and what it takes to succeed. Let's look at the basis on which most sites are built. Here are a few examples, just to give you an idea of what is possible:

Collect Information on a subject

There are many websites that provide information. They were usually started because someone found a lack of that particular information.

If you make a site like this, you can have a forum for discussions, you can have interviews (in writing or videos), quizzes or contests. Monetizing a site like this could be through commercials or sale of products related to the subject of your site.

Express opinions

There are all kinds of "newspapers" providing opinions on specific subjects. These are visited by people interested in that subject. The information and the opinions are often presented as articles with the possibility to discuss the matters.

Typically, these sites will have a comment field under each article. You will always benefit from interaction with people looking for these sites. Discussion are often (but not always) directed to a social media. They are made for easier ways of communicating. Providing enough and "the correct" information, can be a challenge, but if you have great sources, you can make the site everyone wants.

Sell something

Many websites are selling something. Usually products or services that need your special skills. You can sell anything online and there are many website providers that claim to have "the best way" to build an online store.

If you love to test products, you can write reviews on them. If you have a special interest, you can create your business around it. You can write articles or get other people to do it for you. You can offer equal products of different qualities. Products that do more or less the same, but with different prices. Online businesses usually keep in touch with their customers through email for a reason. When people buy from your site, they are more likely to return. If you present your offers to them in an email every now and then, you enhance the chances of their returning.

Teach something

Where do you search when you want to learn something new? On the Internet or in books. Not everyone, but a lot of people do. You can find e-courses or e-books on everything you may want to learn. More and more people start new courses and it is a growing niche on the Internet. If you have some skills you are good at (which of course you have; everybody has something to teach others), you can start an e-course. This is a website where people log in and take the courses.

The above-mentioned ways of making an online business are all basic. You will find all kinds of combinations of these and you may have other ideas on what to do. When you are new, you should start somewhere and expand as you become more skilled. Don't try to do everything at once, you'll lose interest and it will take longer for you to see the results you are looking for. By concentrating on one thing at a time, you get better at what you do and you will know when to move on, when to expand or to start something else. Everything is possible, if you let it.

How you can achieve success in 90 days?

Do you believe you can? First you have to believe it, but there is no need to worry; your focus should be on getting started and then work consistently. Suddenly you have your success, except it won't be sudden, it will be because you know what to do. When you discover what is possible in the next chapter, you will start to see how that actually is possible. There are many tasks you need to do to succeed, but it doesn't have to be as hard as you might think. I want to reveal something very important. To succeed very fast, like in a month or three, there are certain aspects you need to know about. It is possible to succeed fast, but the people who do usually have some advantages most people don't have. Let's take a quick look at the people who succeed quickly and why. They have something in common.

WHO ARE THE PEOPLE WHO SUCCEED FAST?

There are three reasons why people succeed fast:

Number one: they have a natural talent. What that talent is and how it works varies a lot. Just as success is a lot more than we usually associate with the word success.

Number two: they are surrounded by people who can tell them what to do and how to do it, usually good friends or associates.

Number three: they spend a lot of money on coaches, mentors and courses because they see the value they gain and how important it is to always keep learning and working consistently on their business. They are focused and ask a lot of questions and do what they believe in.

What they all have in common, among other things, is that they only focus on one thing at a time. That's more important than you might think at first glance; there is a lot more in that assertion than you can imagine, unless you have experienced it. If you have, you'll soon be the winner, ready to make your online marketing a success. If you haven't experienced it, keep in mind the question of what it means to focus on one thing at a time.

They have understood the power of having the right mindset – not just the power, but also the necessity to succeed. If you work alone most of the time, it gets even more important. We will look into that in many of the other chapters, different aspects you need and why you need them.

When I started, no one taught me this; they gave hints here and there, but a lot of searching, testing and exploring provided me, in the end, with many leads to work on. When I did, I got incredibly stronger, and now I master the skills. They don't master me. It also helps my finances; when you understand these principles, you will understand how you can make the Dollars Want You, instead of you wanting the Dollars.

HOW A WOODEN TERRACE BECAME AN ONLINE BUSINESS

Weeks after I had proudly finished my terrace, constantly using it, enjoying the pleasure of sitting on top of something I build myself, reading books or just letting the sun make my day, making small talk with my family members, while the youngest kids were playing in the yard, it came to me. Just having the good feeling of being alive inside, quietly analyzing what I had done made it quite clear, building an online business is more or less like building a terrace.

It was a solution that made my gardening a lot easier, while an online business was meant to make my income a lot easier. The moment in itself was quite amazing and the resemblances just kept popping up.

When you have your idea, you make a drawing. It's like making a map on how you want everything to fit together. I made a sketch of my website, what it should be about and a few drawings to give myself ideas on what it should look like.

I started to make a list of what I had to do, just like I planned the order in which I had to do the different tasks to build my terrace. When you create a web-site, you want to break everything down in smaller pieces. First you need to find a suitable domain name, then you need to buy it. The next step is to find a host where you can publish your site, then you can start building it. Now that you have bought the materials you need, you may have to learn a bit about them. One thing at a time is recommended.

When you make a foundation for a wooden terrace, you may need to do some digging. You want it level and you want to make sure that surprises don't grow out from underneath it. This is just like making the foundation of your website or business. You want your plan to be as good as possible. You can always change it later, but the happier you are with your plan, the less work you have to put in for the coming changes. Seeing all the possibilities and deciding where to start and building gradually as you get more experienced, is a good idea.

What you are going to promote is of course an important ingredient of the site. When you have decided, it's like building a wooden terrace. First you decide the most important topics and create a webpage for each one of them. The next step is to build one post at a time. A page usually contains a lot of posts. The posts are usually the articles you read on internet, while pages are the main subjects you find in the menu. Creating posts is like placing the planks on the terrace, you do one at a time, make sure it's ok and then continue with the next. Constructing a website should take some time, ideally a never ending story, but it doesn't have to be. However, you don't need to finish it before you start to promote it. You start promoting as soon as you have something to promote. Use what you have, finish the post and you're ready to go.

A terrace needs maintenance; so does a website. When you've finished an article or a page, you are hopefully happy with the results. After a while you might feel the need to make some changes; you should check the need for them and make some changes. This way you make your website gradually look better, your content becomes better and you notice that you are improving. That is a great source of inspiration.

Next best steps!

1. *Search internet for websites matching at least one of your interests. Imagine it was your site. What would you do differently? Look at several sites. You will get many ideas on how to make your site. If you don't find anything you would have done differently, try to go deeper. Look at colors, pictures, fonts and everything on the page. Try to find the answer to why you feel welcome to that site and if you don't, find an answer to that.*

2. *Start reading and deleting your emails. Read them for the sake of learning how to present products, how it communicates with you. Delete them if you don't need them for any-thing. If you feel like buying, try to figure out why. You can use the technique in your emails to your customers. Don't buy into all the products. Work on your critical sense. Look at the prices, but instead of buying the product, save it as a lesson in your library so you can teach yourself how to build your business, your way. It would seem as you bought the product, but you got the money, at least that is a game you should play. Getting used to your new income is a part of getting closer to your success. It's a great way to build what you want your business to be.*

Chapter 2

THE POWER OF ONLINE MARKETING

WHY ONLINE MARKETING IS SO POWERFUL

Imagine that you invest the time you have available and the economic resources you have into your business. If you don't have any money at the moment, don't let it stop you. Start where you are. Right now, it's an image you want to create.

Whatever you have now is what you need to start, and this is the point where you want to grow your business.

The next step is to develop what you need and create everything that you want to fit into your business.

The last step is to get to the point where you earn money.

If you wanted to open an ordinary shop of some kind, you would have to go to the bank, get a loan approved, find someone who could deliver the products you wanted to sell, find a suitable location for your business, decorate it so it looks presentable for your customers, advertise in newspapers and maybe on the radio, as well as talk to a lot of people to let them know what you are doing. These are a few of the things you need to do when you start a business. People who love what they do do it for the happiness they get from creating their own business. They are happy about what they do, so they don't see problems. They are building their future, and they believe in it.

Online marketing is not so different in many ways, but very different in other ways. Let's compare it with the example above. You don't necessarily need a loan. Many solutions for online marketing are free or inexpensive. The products you want to sell may not be so hard to find either. There are possibilities of selling more or less anything at a profit, without even seeing the products (but it is a good idea to know what you are selling). Your products can even be digital. If they are, you create them just one time, and you sell them again and again. Your location is a website. You can design it the way you want. If it is easy to navigate for your customers, they will find the products they are looking for. This makes them happy they found your website, and some of them will return.

There are many ways to advertise a website. You can use newspapers, radio, television, but there are also a lot of ways to do it online. Some are even completely free. As you can see, one of the benefits of starting a business online, or any kind of marketing online, is the fact that you may have everything inside a computer, and the costs can be considerably low. The workload will also be different, even though you have to do much of the same. The major difference is how you run the business. To succeed, you need the same determination and a passionate approach.

Still, people who love what they do do it for the joy of doing it. They are happy about what they do, and they don't see problems. They are building a future they believe in, and so will you.

Great, now we know that expenses can be considerably lower with online marketing than a regular shop, even though the workload in setting up a business might be the same. We also know that running the business is very different, but how it is different, is probably what you are wondering about right now. This is where some of the power of online marketing is hidden.

This happens. When you have set up your business, it's open 24/7. An online business doesn't need to have opening hours. Your customers can be from anywhere in the world and since there will always be someone sleeping while others are awake, it also works the other way around. That's a wonderful thing. You can have customers while you sleep, and the business runs itself. Waking up in the morning and discovering that you have made money while you were sleeping is a good way to start your day.

The Internet consists of many great systems, you are involved in a completely different set of opportunities, because you can have your business run smoothly, while you expand it to the next level or take a vacation.

Wouldn't it be nice to wake up, hear someone speak about the nice weather in Hawaii or Tibet, call the travel agency, order a first class ticket and leave, the same day? It is possible to get there, but it doesn't start there. When you hear about successful people online, you should stop believing that their life was always a success. Like in any part of our society, success has to be made. You create it. The good part is that everyone can create it. You don't need money to become successful, but when you are successful, money seems to become interested in you, so it starts wanting to visit your bank account.

THE POWER INSIDE

This book is about creating your success, and you have taken the first step by searching for it. When you have finished reading this book, you will probably have some of the power you need to start and you will at least have an idea about how to build your inner power. You need your inner power to succeed. Many marketers are very good at using the tools of the trade; they make great websites and everything runs smoothly, but they still don't succeed. Why is this? I discovered on my path to success that some people gave up their search because they had a problem believing. I want to make it clear that your capacity to believe is important for you. Believe in what you believe in – and any higher spirit would want you to believe in your inner power to be the best you that you can be. Never let anyone make you believe that the higher intelligence you believe in wouldn't want you to express yourself as yourself.

Who you are may not even be clear to you. There are so many distractions in our everyday life. It's easy to get confused, lose direction and it can easily make you believe you are who you are now. What you are now is a result of what you have done so far in life. Maybe you were meant for something else? As you read on, you will have the opportunity to find some answers, or more questions. You need to build a strong self; it already exists inside you. It's waiting for you to make the right choices. Maybe you are strong, I don't know you yet, but make it a goal to follow your passion. When you know what it is, you will find a wonderful way of living a lifestyle you want, serving the purpose you are made for and being happier when you finished your work than you are when you're looking forward to the weekends. In a few chapters from here, we will dig deeper into why you want this and how to get there.

We need some tools for our online marketing. You can build the most beautiful business online, but if you don't believe in it, why should other people believe in it?

Let's have a look at the power of the most basic tools, how they enhance your business leverage and then how the tools work.

THE POWER OF THE TOOLS

"You wrote an article on your blog and you see that it has some potential. You make a few adjustments here and there and then you decide it's finished. You publish it. Then you write an email. It's a teaser for the article, just what it is about and why it should be read. You schedule the email to be sent and all the people who have joined your newsletter get the email. Then you write a few words to spread on social media, make it work for the social media you use and share the article along with the teaser meeting the interests of your customers or friends or anyone interested. You glance at your watch

and notice that you have been working slowly today, having spent several hours on your marketing. But the knowledge that you reached several hundred or thousands of people makes up for the effort. You would spend a lot more time if you were to contact each one personally."

I remember it sounded funny when people were talking about the tools. Were they special programs? Did I have to buy them? Where would I find them? I did what I was told, the best way I could, but the fact that they took for granted that people knew about everything made things difficult. I had a lot of troubled nights and days. I had to learn these "tools" and learn them fast. I felt my brain was about to explode at times. Too much information in too short a period of time. That is not healthy. It's not necessary either. You don't have to do things that way, and you shouldn't use that method. It doesn't work. You get very confused and you wind up with a lot to sort out afterwards. You can learn a lot quickly, but you need to do it systematically as it suits YOU, no one else. Your system, the one you build, will change for the better as you go along, so keep your mind open for new tools that seem like a good idea. Very often they are good ideas, but not always.

Every tool has its function, and if you're still confused (*as I was*) about this tool talk, here it is: A computer program you can use in your marketing should now be considered a tool. Any kind of program. That's it. I knew they were programs, but all my human instincts over-complicated everything. You may have a different understanding of this, which is fine, but I know there are others like me, complicating everything. One needs to get used to the fact that computer programs can be called a tool. Actually, it saves time; it takes less time to say tool than to say computer program. It is a Win-Win situation. You need to use another word and it is shorter than the word you usually use. Nothing is better than a time saving, win-win situation; you'll soon start to create win-win situations yourself.

The tools get really powerful when you make them work together. When you send an email, for instance, you can use a tool instead of sending the emails from your personal account. There are online companies who made the service available for anyone. It helps you send the email as it suits you and the way you know your customers want it. You don't have to sit up all night and write a lot of emails. You write the email once, schedule it and send it to your customers the way you want it sent. It is the combination of different tools that makes the biggest difference between a regular store and an online store. When the online tools work together, you can reach incredible numbers of people in a second. This is part of what is called leverage. Leverage is more than that, so let's look into it.

LEVERAGE

"If you master the principles of sword-fencing, when you freely beat one man, you beat any man in the world. The spirit of defeating a man is the same for ten million men. The strategist makes small things into big things, like building a great Buddha from a one foot model. I cannot write in detail how this is done. The principle of strategy is having one thing, to know ten thousand things."
— Musashi Miyamoto

The most important part of the meaning of leverage, is probably the fact that you can use the same content or product over and over again. When you do that, you make it interesting for more and more people, but you only make the content once. The moment you have a product of some sort, you can market it in different ways. The way you present it is the way that people see why they want it or need it. Others' needs are the problems you want to solve. *Your goal is always to make your products so interesting that people see the value in them and are happy when they get them.*

Read that sentence once more and remember it. It is very essential for your coming career.

The more ways you can present a product for different people, the more leverage the product gives you. If you had to buy some services to make the product, you would be able to derive a financial benefit from it based on people deciding to buy it. In the end, your costs may have been covered many times over. When you have a product that sells well, you also get another benefit. People who like what they get, talk about it. The word about your product spreads among people you didn't reach with your marketing. This is also leverage.

Every expense you have on your tools, your marketing, your training and anything concerning your business, should be calculated when you set your financial goals. Think big, but start where you are. Have the end in mind and grow with your business. Your leverage will surprise you one day.

WHAT YOU NEED TO SUCCEED

- The Basic Marketing Tools

WEBSITE

One of the essential tools in online marketing, is the website. There are many different ways of using a website and you use it as it fits the marketing you want to do. There is a big difference between a site that wants to sell you trips and the one that wants to sell you clothes. At the same time, the biggest difference is the appearance. A website is a website, and whether you just want to write a blog or you want to sell fish, the setup is the same in many ways, but these sites would nevertheless look very different from each other. At the same time, this is a powerful quality. If you have a lot of different activities you want people to perform on your site, you can make it suit your needs on different pages on the same site.

The way you choose to present your websitedoes have an impact on your visitors. One of the important aspects of the appearance is how quickly people understand what your website is about. When people are searching for something on the Internet, they hesitate for five seconds before they decide to stay on the site or move on. You have to design your site so that it makes the right people stay on it. It has to balance between what you know attracts people and what you want it to be. This may take some time, but you can learn a lot by studying other websites within your niche.

What language would it be natural for you to use? Language is more than just your native language; you can always make your site as international as possible. The other language is the language that follows what you are marketing. If you are making a website that addresses young people, you should make sure you know how they talk and use the Internet. You want people to feel at home on your website. That's a lot easier if you know how to communicate with the people you want to visit your website. Practice daily until you find what you need to learn. Chat with them often on social media and you'll get there.

THE COSTS

There are two fees you have to pay. The first one is a fee to own the name of your website. This is called a domain. You pay a small fee (annually) for being the rightful owner of the domain name (the name of your site), like *example.com* or *www.example.com*. Example is, of course something you choose. Make sure the name gives a hint about what the site contains. Dollarswantyou.com, for instance, is a website helping people to acquire their online marketing basics, in accordance with this book. The names have to be registered and are considered to be the home of your business. Just like a building (of any kind) has an address, so does a website.

Another annual fee is the hosting fee. This is also a minor, but necessary expense. You might call it rent, like when you rent an apartment. Hosting is exactly the same, only it's for your website. The difference is that you can move your website to another host. It's far more complicated to move the flat.

AUTORESPONDER

Do you remember the email you wrote once and sent to thousands of people? What you are looking for is an autoresponder. You create the content wherever you like, copy it into the autoresponder and send it. It's connected to a list of emails. The list includes the people showing interest in your website. They are subscribers. You can't just add the email addresses you want without permission, but you won't usually do that, either. You present an offer on your website and if they want more information, they sign up. You have probably done the same a few times. A good autoresponder always includes an option to unsubscribe from the list. If you don't want to receive more emails from that company, unsubscribe. Many people subscribe to everything and get annoyed by all the emails they get. This is not the right way of dealing with the situation. It is a lot better to unsubscribe.

When you have a campaign going, you want to send more than one email to your new customers. All of this can be ready long before the customers enter. You can program the autoresponder to send the email to the people who responded to your campaign. This is a very powerful way to run an online business. Another benefit is that you can offer more products later to the same customers (unless they unsubscribed). You want to be nice with your customers so they don't unsubscribe. The best way of doing that, is simply to be nice in the email, make them look at it and give them a chance to consider what you have to offer.

Most autoresponder providers have online courses on how to use their tool optimally. It is a good idea to listen carefully; they know what they are talking about, and they make a living of making it work.

SOCIAL MEDIA - WHAT ARE THEY?

The first thing you need to know about social media is that they are <u>Social</u>. People interacting with other people. Human beings talking to each other without using their voices. The way you communicate is the same way you would communicate if you were standing talking to them face to face. In a pleasant tone of voice, of course.

Social Media are made by people who saw a possibility for new ways of communicating, using the power of the Internet. They are websites or applications where you can interact with people having the same interests as you. You get friends or followers, subscribers. The names are different, but your interaction is the purpose. Being social on your own premises for others to understand who you are and what you do.

Another important aspect of having your business present on social media manifests itself when you release new material. You can "talk" about it on your profile. Letting people know what's on and keeping them updated will probably attract more people to your site. Make sure you don't spam your social media account. Spamming is not interesting for anyone, it just makes you look desperate, which isn't good.

There are a lot more social media in existence than we usually hear of. They all work differently and relate to different people. It's not what you are interested in that is the difference; you will find a personal interest in any of them. The difference is more in how you use the media. Some like sharing content like photos, drawings, stories, while others just like the chat. The social media are built to cover a need and a way to connect to others with similar interests all over the world. (Probably the need of the builder of the site or a need the builder did not find covered.)

WHAT SOCIAL MEDIA IS GOOD FOR MARKETING?

Most social media platforms can be used for marketing. There are very few exceptions. What you choose to market has to target an audience, so your goal is to find an audience having an interest in what you market. Your audience can be anywhere. and that is the problem. You need to find them, so that they can get to know you and your work. You do have a great indicator in the name of the groups you choose, but group names can be confusing. Chat with the people in the group to find out whether it is a good group to search for customers.

The next step is the most critical. You should avoid what many marketers do – they start promoting their offer. Your offer isn't people, so don't do your marketing there. You use the social media to build a relationship with people who share the same interests that you have. When you know them, and just as important, they know you, they are more likely to visit your website. This is your goal. You want them to understand the fact that you know what you are talking about, so they visit your website and subscribe to your email list. They get your offers and they buy them.

Marketing is about sharing your information and getting the people to interact with you. By "fishing" on different social media, you can make them connect with you on the platform where you feel comfortable. Sometimes that works, and you can always find a way to do it.

The best way to reach a large number of people is to advertise on social media. You can direct the commercial to special groups of people and you save yourself a lot of time because you don't have to do all the searches. Most marketers are advertising and they get a lot of subscribers. When you use keywords related to what you market you will get in touch with a lot of people interested in what you market. Many will happily join your email list.

How you like to communicate is one thing; how your audience like to communicate might be another. If you keep communicating differently than your audience on social media, you are making a big mistake. It is normally not you who determines how you communicate on any social media (with the possible exception of that being the fact, of course). Usually there is a mutual understanding of how to behave on each of the platforms. You have to adapt to the language used on the platform you choose to use. This is the reason why it is recommended to start using the ones you already know. Work on being active in your niche (a niche is a group of people, an experienced marketer once said), so people understand you have something of value. This makes them come visit your website. They won't come visiting if you don't respect the people you communicate with. Your good values, should make them want to visit your site, because you represent something of value for them. Give them everything, and they start wanting to give back.

The number of people using the platform does matter. This is one of the reasons why most marketers go for the main social media platforms. If you have an account on one of the most used platforms, you have probably spoken to an online marketer. They are nice people, they don't want to harm you. They like to ask questions and keep the conversation going. A good marketer is interested in what other people are interested in. Why? You want to interact with them. If you show interest in whatever they take an interest in, you are more likely to get a customer sooner or later.

To make sure you find the right platform, you need to know what their purpose is. The most popular platforms are where you meet most people, but make sure you can find customers there. You probably will meet people on all platforms, but some are better for you than others. Start with the one or two you know and try to learn about the others as you get the hang of it.

HOW TO DO SOCIAL MEDIA MARKETING

There are probably thousands of people offering their help on social media marketing. Some know what to do; others tell you what they would have done, hoping it works. The best way to learn this is to join a group and actively connect with people who have the same interests as you.

For the practice, you can start with anything you feel comfortable with. Learning how to make a decent, polite conversation, completely without marketing, is a good idea. Everyone wants to know what you do, and that's the moment you start mentioning your business. Just barely. If they want to know more, find somewhere more private to talk. There are usually possibilities to have a more private chat, or to send messages without publishing them in the open forum. Use it when you talk about your business, and you will maintain respect among the others. They might join you later.

HOW TO LEARN SOCIAL MEDIA MARKETING

I mentioned earlier that there are tons of people who want to teach you how to succeed with social media marketing. Be grateful; listen to what they have to say, but to be consistent in your marketing you should try to keep up with one system. This does not mean you never change, it only means that you change only what doesn't work with the people you want to contact. Everything works, as long as you are kind to others. What you need to learn is how to interact with your audience and the way of communicating that works in relation to them. Another important issue is that you can let these social media interact with each other as a supplement to your website.

You stick to one strategy instead of listening to different speakers saying this while others say that. Killing one's momentum is often the result of using various techniques in the wrong places. As long as you keep to YOUR way of connecting with people on social media, you are more likely to succeed.

VIDEOS

You have probably seen a video online about something you wanted to learn or something you wanted to know. Maybe you just look for funny videos or music videos? They all serve a purpose. Somebody wants you to find it and is happy that you did. Imagine that this was you; you can make it happen. There are many video platforms, and they can be very productive for your online marketing. Videos have a tendency to attract a lot of attention, and for a reason. People are curious. When someone, somewhere, is searching for a video concerning what you offer, you would love for them to find yours.

Videos make a great difference for many websites. People get to know you; they can see you, hear you speak and they get to know you better. This is great for your business. When you are using the videos on your website in addition to the platform, you will reach more people. The more places you find to market what you understand people want, the better.

COMMUNICATION TOOLS

Depending on what kind of marketing you are looking for, there are ways of communicating online that can be very helpful. Using tools where you can chat, talk, phone, share views and more, will help you remain flexible in your business. Many of these services are not necessarily expensive. It's amazing what you can find that will help you build your business. When you are established and make the dollars want you, you will consider buying services. There is always something about the free ones –

they help you, but there are benefits you don't have access to, unless of course you are the creator and you are the one who profits from it.

APP - short for Application

There are more apps than anybody needs, but some of them can be of great help. If you want easy access to something, these small programs can work for you. The first question you should ask yourself is why you want the app. That is the best way to find one that serves you. If you can't find one, you can have it made. There is always someone willing to help you make the app just the way you want it.

There are many companies using their app to release their offers or just to stay in touch with their customers. An app can be a great solution to regularly get people to visit your website when you give a new review, write an article or have a new wonderful offer. You are connected with your customers in a way that makes them feel more welcome, without being pushy.

THE SKILLS YOU NEED TO SUCCEED

PRACTICE YOUR COMMUNICATION

The way you communicate is what keeps you interesting for others. When you write, you want to make sure that people understand what you wish to convey. The moment they feel uncomfortable, they leave. There is always somewhere else they can get what they need. The better you get at communicating, taking their visit serious, the more trust people will have in your work. It's obvious, when you think about it. How often do you return to a shop where the staff yells at you?

PRACTICE YOUR ABILITY TO TYPE

Online marketing might be a bit difficult if you cannot type on a computer. This isn't the only way of doing it, though, but for most people it's the most convenient. If you type something every day, your skills will automatically improve. You will love it when your speed picks up as well. There are courses you could join to learn typing, or maybe you should check what's online?

NEVER UNDERESTIMATE
THE POWER OF SHORTCUTS

There are more ways than one to do anything. When you feel stuck or really don't know what to do, check it out, someone else has always been there; they solved the problem and made a video. Unless they just wrote a blogpost. Making it a habit to search for what you need is a real time saver. You might wonder why I call it a skill; it's simply because you should practice searching often, then you get better at searching and spend less time searching and more time learning.

Another benefit is what you can do with the shortcut you learned. If you write an article about it, you may also make a video, where you show how to use it. When you publish both, making sure that your domain name (website address) is easily spotted, you not only help other people with a problem, you are promoting your website and yourself. People get to know you in this way and when people know who runs the business, they are more likely to buy the products or at least visit your website. Any problem can be a gate to a new customer, this way. Being helpful is a good idea.

THE BASICS OF THE TOOLS

Your tools should be your dearest friends when you do your online marketing. The better you are at using them, the more they help you. There is also the fact that the better you know your tools, the more time you save.

When a tool is new to you, you should take some time just to see what it can do. You don't have to learn everything at once, but the more you know of what it can do, the better you understand how and when it can help you. The other benefit this provides you is the knowledge of what it doesn't do. Then you don't have to waste time searching for it in that tool. No matter how natural you think it is, if it's not there, find it somewhere else.

THE KNOWLEDGE YOU WANT TO HAVE

A great part of finding what you believe in and how you can profit from it, is that you are constantly looking for news about it. You want to know as much as possible, and you want to share it. Most people search for information on the Internet. You probably do too, and I'm no exception either. If you already know the answer, your website should contain it. Especially all the topics concerning the topic you present on your site. Search engines have a liking for websites that grow. The more material your website contains, the better it will rank on search engines. A search engine is simply a computer giving you the sites containing what you are searching for. If you search for purple dogs, you will get a lot of sites saying something about it. When you know what a purple dog is, you can use it in your marketing.

You become a specialist in your interest, if you constantly read about it, talk about it, listen to what others have to say, get different opinions on the matter. The only limitations are those you set yourself. You can find what you are looking for because you search for it; then make it your own in a way the others don't mention. This way you get a reputation of being one of the people who have the answers to the problem. That is what people are looking for. The more you know, the more content you produce, the more people will find your website.
This isn't done in a day, but if you constantly work on your content, your site will rank higher. When your site is new, you share what you have on social media and other people like it, they share it and hopefully this will attract more and more people. The more knowledge you have, the better.

Not every site works like this. Some sites are meant for other things. They should still contain as much material as possible. You never know when you have enough material to be seriously ranked. The more consistent, and the more daily effort you invest, the bigger your chances become.

When you have answered all the questions you deem necessary, it's time to make sure you learn about all the other things related to your interests. The more your visitors find, the more your site will be visited. Nothing is perfect from the start. In the beginning there is nothing, you start with what you have and build it from there. Don't do it mainly for others, keep your passion up and do it for your own pleasure. The more you give, the more you get.

Everything of interest can be a new source of income. Your way of presenting the material can also make it profitable. The best way of learning about that is to visit sites you like. See what they do and follow their example. There is a time for copying, but no time to paste. Make it your own, and you will begin developing your own way of making the website profitable.

It's important to accept that you already have some knowledge that others don't have. What is obvious for you can be the exact information for which others have been searching for years. Expand your knowledge beyond what you know and remain confident in your own growth. Then your business will reward you for a journey you couldn't imagine.

YOUR MINDSET IS YOUR POWER

"You cannot make an omelet without breaking eggs"

Your mindset, is your friend. It's an important part of you. The way you treat your mindset is the way you manage everything you do. If you are having a wonderful life, then you probably have a healthy mindset.

Why do you say "probably have"?

Your mind is exposed to a lot of things during the day. It keeps you safe. When something happens, your brain constantly considers the danger in it. If you hear a new sound, have you noticed what you do? Your brain makes you turn in the direction where the sound came from. It wants you to see what made it. When you do, you know if it's good or bad. You have learned something. We learn something new every day, even without paying attention to it. When you are aware of all the wonderful things your brain does for you, and you know how to turn everything in your favor. You have a strong mindset. First, you need to get rid of all the noise made by all the conversations you've had, everything negative has to go. Gossip, for instance, is not good for a healthy mindset; it makes you unclear of what you are capable of. You start wondering about what they say about you when you're not there. When you have a strong mindset, you don't care. You know why you do what you do, and you stick to it because it works.

When you start your marketing, you are where you are. You have to acknowledge the fact that the life you have lived has resulted in what you are right now. If you want to do something else, you have to change something. You can try to change a lot of things, like habits, friends, you can move to another country if you wish, but if you keep the same mindset, you will stay who you are. I don't say you are bad or evil or even that it's wrong not to change. You can be the nicest human being on earth, but if you want to do something new, you also need to prepare your mindset for what is new.

The stronger you are, the better solutions you get. Your mind brings them to you, when you make it understand what you are looking for. This is very fortunate when you are in the making of something that matters for you. You will experience good and bad days. Challenges occur, but if you can trust yourself, you will know that the solution will turn up when you need it. You have probably experienced this many times already. When was the last time you desperately needed an answer, and suddenly someone tells you or it just popped up in your head? You have experienced it, and you have it in you. It's there, ready for you to take the right actions.

THE RESCUE HABITS AND TOOLS

When everything feels wrong, it's great to have ways of solving the problems. One by one. Sometimes it take days, but as long as you have a set of tools that work, you know you will find what's wrong, change it and you can move on.

There are tools for anything, and when you work on your mindset, you will also discover that you can change the situation easily with the right tools. It's not a matter of taking a tablet and waiting for it to pass, it's about letting go of what is stopping you. Many of the habits we have and the beliefs we have are holding us back from what we want to do. They are called limiting beliefs. They can be hiding everywhere inside us, not really serving us, but preventing us from doing whatever we want to do.

There are many ways to get rid of limiting thoughts but first you have to find them. Many methods can help you find them and get rid of them. You will probably be surprised when you find what keeps you from who you really are. There is a lot of truth in "life works in mysterious ways." The fun part is that this is not a mystery, it's nature. We live in a world full of technology, but our mind and body are still a part of nature. Easy to forget, but interesting to explore.

A great way to start working on your mindset and to learn about limiting beliefs, is to start watching motivational videos. If you never looked at one of those, they might seem a little weird or worse. Don't worry, they are not. They might say a few things you don't believe in, well, time to find out if it is a limiting belief or not.

HOW TO MAKE DOLLARS WANT YOU ONLINE

1. **Pick your interest.** *Just One. It has to be something you can work on for a longer period without getting tired of it. You need to have an interest in what you do, if you don't, it would simply take too much of your energy.*

2. **Search the Internet for products** *that are interesting for other people with the same interest as you have. These products can be your new income or a lesson in how to promote yours.*

3.   **Make yourself a website.** *If you don't know how to do that, there are tons of free website builders online. Look for one that provides all the training you need.*

4.   **Make space to work on your website.** *Daily effort is preferred, but if you have to skip a day, then you can incorporate that into your plan. Weekly is also better than never, but it will also take a lot more time to start making the money.*

5.   **Make a plan for how your site should develop.** *Knowing what comes next is a very good idea. You should also have a "sacred" time for your weekly adjustment of your plan. The longer time you plan for, the better.*

6.   **Learn something new every day.** *You already do, but becoming aware of what you learn can make your website reach far beyond your expectations and it certainly helps keeping your focus on your goals.*

7.   **Spread the good word** *(your business, your products, your posts) on all the social media you can possibly think of. Well, at least those read by the people who want to buy what you have to offer.*

8.   **Chat, speak, write, discuss with the people around you,** *in real life and online. Keep to your mission (your interest) and you get a lot more help in spreading the word (your golden shop online). ... Just don't overdo it. If all you talk about is you and*

your business, they might lose interest. Let the conversation benefit both parties, get equal and win the new customers.

9. **Don't be disappointed** *if you don't sell anything at first. You need to develop your relationship with your customers. Be happy for your own activity and do your best at all times. (Which is the best way to continually improve).*

10. **Celebrate the small successes.** *They are a great preparation for your bigger successes. Success follows the people who keep doing what they do. If you quit, start over, quit, start over, quit, start over (could be continued forever...) you confuse people. Instead you should start, adjust a little, continue, adjust a little... (to be continued forever) and the result is a lot of small successes along the way. Anything can be presented in a way that makes it natural combined with anything else. The only limit is your imagination. If you don't have any imagination, YET, it's time to wake it up.*

11. **Believe in yourself.** *If you don't - why should anyone else? There is no one who knows you better than yourself. You are the only one who has been there every second of your life. Don't let anyone convince you that they know better. They might bring helpful advice, but they can't tell you what you think is right. Others' limiting beliefs have stopped a lot of talented people. Don't become one of them.*

YOU CAN DO ALL OF THIS
- IT AWAITS YOUR ACTIONS

These are the first tasks you have to do. You don't actually have to do it, you can buy every service you want. There is always a website ready to help you with your needs and tasks, but in the end, if you spend all the money you have, you will discover that online marketing can be expensive in many ways. Being aware of what you should pay for and what you can do yourself is important to succeed. You have to work with the balance of everything. This doesn't mean to sit in your cage of comfort and hope for the best. You are a winner when you challenge yourself, even if you "fail".

Failure is only a failure if you stop or you don't learn anything from it. If you stop, you have failed. If you learned something, you gain an experience, and you do want experiences. You can even profit from that experience. Money goes where it is wanted and if you paid someone but didn't get what you really wanted, someone is in trouble, but it's not you. Let everyone have their trouble, while you see the challenge in yours. In this case, you want to understand it like this; Your money pleases someone else, you get the experience. You share that experience and if you play your cards right, money from other people will want you.

The best part of online marketing is the learning part. You need to learn new skills and as you do, you will find that you are smiling more often. It looks wonderful, by the way, your smile. Get used to it, it's your friendly you.

"Twenty years from now you will be more disappointed by the things that you didn't do than by the ones you did do. So throw off the bowlines. Sail away from the safe harbor. Catch the trade winds in your sails. Explore. Dream. Discover."

- Mark Twain

Next best steps!

Take some time to reflect on how you believe you would have a wonderful time, marketing online. You don't have to be afraid of failing, just imagine what you feel would be your way of doing it. This exercise makes your brain work on what would be better for you. There is an answer, and you have it inside.

You may use these questions to support you and make sure you get started:

1. *What kind of marketing is best for you?*

2. *Is there any kind of marketing you do not want to do? (if you find some, write down why and explain it).*

3. *What kind of marketing did you find most interesting when you searched for websites (chapter 1)?*

4. *What do you need to do to learn this?*

5. *How would you set your goals and schedule them? (don't leave the chance to actually test it, you might even come up with a great idea).*

[77]

6. *Imagine that you reached your goal. How would you celebrate it and thank everyone involved?*

Over the next few days, you should work on this story. Just let your mind wander, write it down if you want (practice typing?), make sure you smile, it's a game, and you will probably surprise yourself. If not, try to, it helps in more ways than you know. Here's a suggestion for the title (have a better idea? Use it):

A GREAT DAY FOR ME AS AN ONLINE ENTREPRENEUR

Chapter 3

HOW TO TURN YOUR PASSION INTO PROFIT

.... drowsy in front of the television. Something is rolling over the screen, I do not know what it is, but my eyes are captivated by the action, sometimes a lot, other times almost no action at all. I considered turning it off, but there was still some action, someone moved something and other people entered the screen, changing the action, sometimes fast, sometimes very slow. Suddenly it got to me; this was not the same program. I was watching another program. This was a completely different one, with a story about something else. It had probably started some time ago, I didn't know. Nor did I know what the story was either, but drowsy as I was, it became too much to press the button to make it stop. It was easier to let it stay turned on than to turn it off. In the middle of the night, I woke up, on the couch. The television was still on. I got to bed, hoping the next day had something better to offer...

I didn't make up that story. It actually happened. I didn't like it. I had to do something. I had to find my life. I started by turning off the television and have barely watched it since.

Most people have what they call a dream. Most people let it be a dream and only a dream. I read some research on people at the end of life speaking about their regrets. Most people were happy about all the things they had done, for different reasons, of course. The only regrets they had were the things they didn't do. I made the decision that my life was not going to end like that. I wanted a life I couldn't regret.

Why do we all look forward to the weekends?

Searching for a better self and looking for the best way of living life the way it's best lived is quite ordinary. I'm sure you could find some of your friends doing just that, without telling anyone. It's private. The search is private; you are touching the nerve of your own path in life, and no one should mess it up. That is why we keep it private. When we get closer to a result, start seeing the outcome of the search, something happens. You will notice, if you haven't already.

Why are you doing exactly what you are doing? That question was one of those first questions I asked myself. It's funny what happens when you start listening to yourself after asking that question. I know I'm not alone looking for the answers, and I'm not alone in finding some of the answers, but I am the only one who can make the changes needed for me to fulfill what I will call "A Life Well Lived". So are you. You are the only one who can tell yourself how you should live your life, to call it a life well lived when someone asks you how your life has been. Do you have a plan?

Do This Now:
Repeat to yourself (a couple of times):
"I am the only one who can tell __me__ how to live my life to call it "A Life Well Lived". I take responsibility now. Every day in every way, I'm getting better and better!"

WHAT IS PASSION AND HOW TO FIND YOURS

"The two most important days in your life are the day you are born and the day you find out why."
— Mark Twain

Living your life on your own terms and doing whatever you feel like doing is a dream we all have. Our dreams are changing as we keep on living, but there is one, a bigger dream about life, which never changes. Your life purpose, what you are made for, what you are best at.

You may say; "Dream on". Well, that's exactly what you shouldn't do. It's time to take action and arouse your curiosity.

Can you hear yourself saying; "What if it isn't just a dream? Maybe it is what I am supposed to do."
What is your answer?

When Mahatma Ghandi wanted to free his people, he took the actions needed to make it happen. Then he travelled back home and started to free his people. It doesn't matter if your dream is as big or a lot smaller, your dream is worth checking out. The worst that can happen is you having a wonderful journey through your own life, not finding the results you wanted. It can be better, it can be different, but most important is that you are searching.

There is a saying: "Life is what happens while we are busy doing other things." If you don't believe you have the right to a wonderful life, this is it. Life is what happens while you search for your better life. When you find it, you also see a new path that looks even more exciting. You reach your goals and you see that trail of a new exciting path, you take the challenge and start the new journey. The line of opportunities is endless. You will never have a boring day in your life, unless you choose to. How this applies to you is exactly the same that applies to me and everyone else.

I do have some natural talents. You have some natural talents. I love music and I love working with music. You love something (state it; "I love ......") and you love working with it.

Implementing new ways of working with music is easy for me. I have focused a lot on getting better at it (for years), so I am better at it now than I used to be. I also love working with people. I'm having a very good time when I can combine those two. It's a combination of two skills I've spent a lot of time and lots of money to develop. I never saw it as money spent, I still see it as an investment into a better life.

You have your talents. We don't always know what our talents are. If you haven't found your talent, you have something great to look forward to. Your talent is there, even without you knowing it, because you don't see it as a talent. You are good at something, and it gives you a great feeling dealing with it.

I have had my success in different areas of my life. I'm grateful for all the help I have got from a lot of friends and other friendly people who have helped me to succeed. I am certain that you have experienced the same. You always remember those moments when ...

What is your talent?
What is your passion?

There are periods of my life where I have been working days and nights to learn some new skills and follow what my curiosity told me to follow. Some of these periods have been very exhausting, but others have been exciting. There's nothing to wonder about. You just love those moments; they mean something.

Life is about learning something new that makes your coming days better and more exciting. I've found myself learning weird things, completely without a clue why. Later it has shown itself to be very handy. Being open to learning something new, may be a part of the preparation of your future.
When you love what you do , live the lifestyle you choose and have a deeper understanding of why you do it. You have found your passion. Your way of living your life, just the way you want. This is very powerful when you start your online marketing. This is what makes you a success.

START YOUR PASSIONATE SEARCH FOR YOUR PASSION – NOW

What you are about to do is get into your dreams and search for the right answers in life. Your life. You will experience questions turning up in your head. You should write them down. You want the answers. You will experience mood changes, days of laughter and despair. Laugh and enjoy the excitement of your many moods. In the end, you will find what you are looking for.

You probably have an idea of what this can be. As you get used to what you experience, you want to go deeper. It's a fascinating journey and it's free of charge. There are ups and downs, but you control them more and more as you go along.

I have seen a lot of these exercises, but I found a problem that usually occurs. They often start by asking you to imagine that you have all the money in the world, all the success you wanted and complete control of your life. What are you doing and how did you get there?

Your answer is; "I Don't Know, I Don't Have The Answer!" (you should say YET, here). You might feel the anxiety coming crawling, telling you "Why should I know, I can't imagine that." Now is another good time to add; YET! Try now.

WHAT YOU ARE LOOKING FOR, WITHOUT KNOWING IT

The method I'm introducing you to below, is different. This is my version. It helped a lot to get rid of all the noise we are surrounded with. Noise is everything that turns your thoughts away from You. House, bills, car, friends, family, activities, the lawn (if you have one), your clothing, your inadequacies, your friends' envy of what you have, your attitude toward what you are doing and so much more. Some of these are called limiting beliefs (and if you say "but I like that", it probably is a limiting belief, and if you feel I'm rude by saying just that, I'm sorry to say you have discovered one of your limiting beliefs), which you want to get rid of.

There is a time for everything; you will find more about the limiting beliefs in Chapter 6, but now is a good time to introduce you to "The Caveman Method". I'm sure you are curious about who you really are. You will get ahead of thousands of people in your online marketing just by *searching* for those answers. Now, let's introduce:

THE CAVEMAN METHOD

"I have no faith in human perfectibility. I think that human exertion will have no appreciable effect upon humanity. Man is now only more active - not more happy - nor more wise, than he was 6000 years ago."
- Edgar Allan Poe

INTRODUCTION

Poe refers to the start of the Mesopotamian culture. Let's go further back in time; 170 000 years and then get back from there. (170 000 years is chosen for the sake of decency. This is the time scientists say that homo sapiens like you and me started to wear clothing). All they had was a cloth. There is of course a discussion as to whether they lived in caves or not. In this case it is the term, cavemen (and women), that is in our interest. None of us would exist without the women, we are very grateful for them, giving us all birth.

Humans as cavemen indicates that they had nothing at all. There is nothing other than the opportunities nature has to offer. The important thing is that you are alive. What kept you alive is a very good start to explore how you can be what you want to be.

This is an exercise, and you don't have to be a caveman all the time, you can switch between now and then, as you wish. The importance of starting with nothing is to get rid of all distractions our present life has to offer. There are thousands of distractions, but when we focus on what is important, which is You, without anything else (keep the cloth on and you'll be fine), you will get closer to what you are searching for.

You may not manage everything in this exercise the first time you try, but when you repeat it, preferably daily, you will be amazed by what you will experience. If you do this everyday, starting from scratch, consistently for 30 days, you are probably very close to an answer you have been looking forward to finding.

FOCUS ON THE OUTCOME

The tasks may be practiced anywhere, inside, outside, when you walk, when you sleep. As long as you focus on the outcome, it should work fine. The amount of time you spend on these exercises, is up to you. It's recommended to spend at least 15 minutes a day, at least every now and then when it occurs to you that you actually have a great future. Just imagine what you want; that is your outcome. If you have the chance to repeat the exercise one or more times during the day, you should. Have fun with the way you perform the exercise and you will get amazing results too. The outcome, the results, will be clearer and you'll succeed faster. If you really want some changes, but keep doing what you always have done, why would you expect a different result? Get it? Have fun, laugh more, enjoy the game, live life. Changes are needed to make something different. You can start now, nothing to dwell on, it will only get better, then better and then even better. Good and bad days will come, but you will understand why, when you start. Now, is always a great time to start. If you keep on reading, everything will reveal itself one day or just suddenly.
Ready for action?

Here we go!

In the beginning - there was you
Imagine yourself having nothing else than a piece of cloth to protect you from the cold. You are standing on a field of grass, barefooted, the temperature is perfect and you feel wonderful.

Task 1 - You

Let's focus on you. Don't bother about the others; they're fine:

1. Who are you and how do you look?

You are one of the most important cavemen. Maybe you are admired for your skills; maybe you are admired for some actions you took. You know who you are, and why you are admired (the fun thing in the exercise is that it could even be because you are very good at using your computer, decorating your house, gardening, knitting, thinking, procrastinating, sleeping, walking, creating waves, dinners, love frogs, princes or princesses. Have fun!).

Action: *Imagine yourself being there. You don't have to see yourself clearly, maybe you can feel the wind, the heat of the sun, hear the grass whispering in the warm wind, smell all the wonderful scents of nature.* **Close your eyes and feel, see, hear or smell the environment. Why do they admire you? How do you see yourself being admired?** (you may want to use a mirror, to help imagine yourself)

2. How do they see you?

You are feeling wonderful, but you are not alone. There are some people around you, they can be your family, friends or others. They are very important to you and they are friendly people.

Action: *Imagine being one of the others looking at you having a wonderful time. Try to get a scent of the environment, hear all the sounds (are there birds?), feel* *the wind, the temperature and all the people having a good time, chatting, laughing in this great area. **Close your eyes, imagine you are one of the others. Feel, see, hear and/or smell the environment while you see how they see you.***

3. The environment
- what is your favorite?

Let's change the scenario. Change where you are located, but stick to the nature and the people; there is no need for anything else, yet. Keep the image of the people, switch from you looking at them and one of them looking at you having a great time.

Action: *Imagine being in your favorite environment with the most important people in your life. Feel it, smell it, hear it and admire the view from where you are, having fun. (You admire the people around you as they admire you), What are you doing when you have fun? **Close your eyes and feel, see, hear, smell the environment, enjoy the good feeling.***

GREAT WORK!

Now you should start feeling good. How far you got in your imagining doesn't matter. It will improve when you repeat this task. You don't have to believe it, but it will improve when you repeat this task. Remember this: "Every day, in every way, I'm getting better and better". (Yes, I know, I repeated that sentence intentionally; it is that important.)

YOUR IMAGINATION

You should have an idea of who you are after the first task, if you don't, it's just a matter of time. By repeating the exercise, you'll improve the idea, and you get used to seeing yourself as the self you want to be when you are having a good time as in successful, or being a winner. If you feel stuck, don't worry, it doesn't help; it just makes things worse and produces more worry material. You don't need the worry material anymore; let it go, it doesn't serve you. Use your idea of yourself. Place yourself in your favorite environment; make sure you have a good time.

Hungry? Even cavemen had to eat and drink. The right food gives us the right nutrition. They didn't know this, but ate what they felt like eating. We tend to get confused on this. We need to eat the food that gives us the necessary power to stay alive and handle every situation properly.

Primitive man, like the caveman, was driven to find a way to find food. He was forced by his consciousness of necessity.

"I want food," said primitive man. This drove him to activity and led to his unfoldment, for it awakened in him a consciousness of his ability to supply that want. It led him to recognize the fact that food already existed. He did not, however, reach our higher viewpoint."
What Henry Harrison Brown wants us to understand with these words, is the fact that we do lots of things because we have to. There is no way to avoid it; we just have to do it to get what we want. When we want

something badly enough, we change our focus to be around what we want. Later he mentions that this want comes from necessity, which keeps our attention occupied on the wrong things, the want and the necessity. We work on the progress, keep our attention on the progress and lose track of why we are in the progress. The end result.

Imagination caused a huge change even for cavemen. By drawing their lives and their actions on the wall in the cave, they also started to see how and why it worked. The progress became the tool to get there, not the primary goal.

Task 2 - Your Skills

This task is about taking action. There are certain things you would take immediate action to solve.

1. Hunger

You are hungry. You have no food. Luckily, you are the clever one in the tribe. You know the tribe (if you are a woman) and/or you know the hunters (if you are a man). Either way, you have something they want so badly, they hunt food for you as well as for themselves and their families. You have great ideas, you know how to present it for the hunters and you get a lot of attention because of it. What are these skills and what knowledge is this?

Action : *What is it you imagine yourself doing that attracts a lot of people and makes them feel attracted to you? How can anything you are good at become a way to attract them to you? Even the craziest ideas are* important here. Write them down on a piece of paper. Let them grow, while you have fun with the rest of the exercises, even if it's just in your mind.

2. Time Spent
How do you spend your time when you attract all these people (or attract this attention)?

Action: *Imagine yourself doing what you are good at. Write at least the keywords on a piece of paper while you imagine yourself in action.*

3. What Do You Like?
Which of these activities that you see yourself doing do you like? Which are the ones you do not like?

Action: *Sort them in likes and dislikes (you can add a plus or a minus sign over the keywords, sentences, your story or whatever you wrote under the second question).*

4. Use Your List Of What You Like.
If these were the tasks that you should do, what could you make of it? What outcomes result when you only do what you like?

Action: *Write down anything you can imagine and more. Everything is of interest here. If you see something you need to be better at to manage, write it down. It's a part of you. If in doubt, write it down. Never, as in NEVER, hesitate to write it down.*

NOW, that you have performed these four actions, taken the time to imagine yourself, why others see your potential, where you are supposed to be and doing what you like to do (maybe what you are passionate about), there is just one task left in this exercise, namely the fifth: your future.

First, let me tell you a story from the beginning of the twentieth century. In Egypt, they found a lot of the tombs of the ancient Egyptian Kings. They were all empty, due to plundering, but one man kept digging. He still had the hope that he would find something of importance. He read every theory, every anecdote, not leaving anything to chance. He discovered, not by chance, the tomb of Thut-Ank-Amon, the only royal grave intact. Carter's intuition, just knowing there had to be something, paid off. He found what no one else found – a royal tomb, with all the treasuries present. He didn't even consider World War I as an obstacle. He continued, the day he was able to. He started where others had been digging for ten years, without results...

You never know when success will arrive, but if you believe, you will find the answers.

Here's the fifth action:

5. Your Future

Ten years from now, your success will have already been a fact for most of those years. What is it that you are drawn to that makes you keep going, with the same enthusiasm you had when you started?

Action: *Write down the story. Tell it to yourself. Remember to include your lifestyle and why it is so great to live the life you want to live. How does your life benefit other lives and why is your work so interesting that people are still drawn to what you do.*

CONGRATULATIONS

Your passion is close to you! Success is not about money; it's about passion. This is true for online marketing just as much as it is true for any other success. Money is only a way of changing services between people. Money is a tool. They cannot do anything without you giving them the direction to make you more money. Your next goal is to make sure that you are so attractive that Dollars want you. When you do what you are good at, in a way that attracts people, you don't need money; you don't want money. Dollars want you, because you know how to deal with them and you give something back.

DOLLARS WANT YOU

"Poles of Thought.

Having acquired the proper mental attitude, there is something necessary for you to do to draw the Dollar. Your magnet of desire must have two poles. First, you must have something which the world needs and is willing to pay for. In this respect you must follow the law of supply and demand. You must honestly feel that you will give the Dollar's worth of every Dollar that you desire. Secondly, you must, in all sincerity, dedicate every dollar that comes to you to noble service. You can then feel that Dollars want you; that through them you can give what you have of value to the world. Feel that Dollars wish you to use them for the accomplishment of your purpose to use them justly. With this ideal, you can conscientiously invite Dollars and they will come. They need your heart, brain and hand that they may benefit the world."

- Henry Harrison Brown

Essential about money: when you give people your money, they become happy. Their happiness spreads to other people. Other people get happy. In the end, this means that you will be happy and you will receive more than you gave away, because you started something and it will get back to you. Maybe in a different shape and value, but giving is a great way of starting a career as whatever you like.

When it comes to money, I've started taking an interest in it, and the knowledge I have achieved over the years by not being interested is coming in very handy. There are so many ways to monetize knowledge, sometimes I don't quite know which one to follow next.

This particular interest, learning about money, really had me thinking about how to perform the right actions in the right order. Money works in mysterious ways, people say, but there is not as much mystery as we want to believe. There is more of the wrong attitude and understanding of money than there is mystery.

There are trillions of dollars in the system waiting for you to attract them. There are only billions of people, so there should be enough for everyone. You are no exception.

MONEY - THE GOOD AND BAD

Every dollar has two sides. Dealing with money makes people nervous, so money is easily seen as a necessity, but we don't really like it, it's good for one thing and bad for another. There is a balance. The dollar itself is not good or bad, it is neutral, but the way the way we use it makes us feel good or bad. So far, so good. Then we transfer those feelings to the money, which makes the money good or bad. If we look at the dollar and accept it as a balanced mean of switching services, we can make the difference that makes our business more interesting than the others.

Imagine this:
If one side was good and one side was bad, the dollar itself would be in perfect balance. You know people get happy when you give them your money, and you get happy if people give you money. The good side is easy to understand and accept. The other side, the bad side, is merely following the good side. They are still equal. What you want is to make the change of money more positive than negative and this has to do with the actions you take beyond the money.

When you accept a dollar (or any amount), there is an expectation in the person you got it from. This person may expect that your business is done, and you don't have to be in touch anymore. There is a balance and it's all right, but not more than that. It's neutral.

If you give something else to that person, something the person needs, something that improves the life of the receiver, then you are giving something that has more value than was expected for the amount. The balance is not neutral, it is positive. This balance makes the other person look upon you as a good person, tells others about this something and others want to give you their dollars as well, expecting to get the same something to improve their lives. This is a win-win situation. You help other people and they help you by telling other people about it. Dollars want you, because you treat them well.

Sometimes when you give people your money, they have told you that you will get the help you need. You get the service, training or product, but you don't feel you get the help or service you need. You become disappointed and you feel like you have paid more than you gained. In this situation, the balance is negative. You will not run around telling how great it was to receive this product; on the contrary, you are not interested in keeping in touch with this person. This service, training or product doesn't serve you. The negative balance taught you a lesson; the other person got the money, but there is a negative balance. This needs to be dealt with. You can't go around dwelling on the situation. You wish to find what to learn from this and make sure that you don't get in this situation.

Turn this part of this story around and imagine yourself being the one delivering a product that is inadequate. You wouldn't get the good vibes in the situation; most people won't tell you about it, so all you experience is that dollars don't want you, because you don't treat them well. You don't give them a good reputation. They will not bring more of their friends to you.

Your passion makes you proud of what you do, but pride doesn't help here. Your task is to keep up the good work, doing what you are good at, and keep on improving it. Share what you love to do, talk about it in a way that makes people happy and make sure they get more value than they pay for. This doesn't mean giving away everything for free, but it means that what you give is of more value than what they pay for. You can deliver something worth thousands of dollars for the price of thousands of dollars and still have a great business. Your attitude and the way you act will determine whether people buy it or not. The right price and your values makes dollars want you, because you respect them and make them do a great job for you by bringing a lot of their friends your way.

BE AWARE OF WHAT YOU DON'T WANT YOUR MONEY TO DO

Dealing with money can be a hard task. When you do your marketing and you are searching for answers, you will notice the tension, the suspicion and a lot of thoughts about legal issues. Online marketing has a reputation of not necessarily being the most trustworthy place to do marketing. People who claim this, are usually very afraid of anything online, very careful with everything in their lives and have more than enough just trusting the people that surround them.

There is nothing wrong with those people; they just haven't found the safety they need in their lives. There are many reasons for these rumors about online marketing and some of the reasons are actually started by people who want to do good. This is very confusing, but when you have worked on your mindset and you know what it takes, you are also able to stay away from the sites that wish well, but harm more than they help.

There are more reasons than this book will discuss, but the important message here is to keep up your willingness to learn, and you will be an expert in finding what works and how it works.

Thousands of programs are waiting to recruit you. Some are good and some are bad. The good ones offer you training of some kind, for a reasonable price. The bad ones may offer you some kind of training, but they fail to follow up on your development. It's not easy to say which one is good and which is bad. You need to do some research and don't be fooled by the timers. Just refresh the page and you start all over again (at least in most cases).

The get-rich quick-programs are usually the worst. The tempo is high and everyone is nervous. You are told to act fast so you can start earning money NOW. Usually people don't start earning money at all. Lately a few of these programs have begun to take their training very seriously, you even get a coach. This is a good idea, but you still have to pay monthly fees for something you may not be ready for the next year. What you get is based on their experience, it works, but since you don't know what you will find in your search for your passion, what you have to do to make it possible, you may spend a lot of money for nothing. I don't want to scare you; there's probably no need for alarm. I wouldn't say be careful, but I would say, consider the situation from your position, not the one they want you to be in; namely, the desperate, "act now or you lose thousands of dollars" attitude. They lose money if you do not join, but you lose money if you do. You should consider what you need to learn before you want to join any company with a monthly fee. Then you will enter and make it a win-win situation, they get your money and you can use their experience because you know what it takes, so you can build your successful business.

There is a lot of tension in conjunction with many online companies, unfortunately very often based on limiting beliefs. This makes the whole situation very interesting and very delicate. Dealing with money does something to people, and you will quickly notice that if you don't make money, your friends won't come and visit you, at least not easily. When you have made money, your friends will treat you naturally and you will also behave decently, properly, friendly, the best a human can be to other humans.

You want to listen carefully to what they say. There are two main reasons. You should know what you don't want to do with your money, or to put it another way, what your money should do. When you are looking for an opportunity that suits you, you should be aware of what you want. The best way of becoming aware of what you want is actually to start with the complete opposite. Start by being aware of what you don't want.

When you have listened to what they say, it's time for you to check out what they didn't say. This is the first reason why you need to listen carefully. When you get an offer that sounds fantastic, check the details, what kind of work does it take, what kind of skills are needed (they often say none, but don't just take their word for it, check it out), what kind of training do you get. What does it really cost? Are there many levels of payment? Ask them. If you don't get the answers, you may have found someone hiding something, check it out.

Imagine yourself enter a restaurant you've never been to. There is no menu. You ask the waiter about the food and all they will tell you is that you can eat it. Would you be happy with that?

... and if you want to buy a car, would it be all right if all they told you the price of the steering wheel and nothing else? I believe you would like to know exactly what you need to pay for the whole car, not part by part, but the whole car, when you buy it. This is the other important reason why you need to listen carefully. The way they represent it teaches you how to present what you are looking for. If you like it, you can use it; if you don't like it, don't use it. Every experience you have in your search for how to design your online marketing includes a lesson.

My experience shows that the more the company gives in value, such as free samples, the more reliable customers they get. It's quite normal to give your email address as a payment for the free sample; it's the way any online business can keep in touch with their customers. If you don't want to receive any more of their offers, you can always unsubscribe. Every email you get from a company, any size, should contain an option to unsubscribe or change your subscription.

Unfortunately, there are companies based on the concept that you pay for a service, they take your money, you do the job and you take the risk. If you get in touch with any such company, you want to consider that risk before you join. Sometimes it's all right, but not always. If they tell you to act very fast, they are probably afraid that you won't take the offer. Keep an open mind, train your mindset to alert you, check the details and then make a decision based on what is good for you and serve you.

BE AWARE OF WHAT YOU WANT YOUR MONEY TO DO

Your passion is your friend, your spark in any situation. You are looking forward to work on it, deal with it, talk about it and create a wonderful life for yourself. These are all positives. They make you happier and you feel alive. It's good to feel alive when you live. I would say it feels natural.

When you are searching for ways to activate your business, you will experience some doubt, a lot of questions and many suggestions. This can be very confusing. This is why it is a great idea to make sure you have a notion about what you are looking for. Just starting to look without knowing what you want easily enables you to choose the wrong solution, be excited by the wrong offers and spend a lot of money on things you don't need or cannot learn from. You're right, you do learn something: what to avoid, the expensive way. This can create some anger, and worst case scenario is that you give it all up. You go back to step Zero, grow old, get bitter and make life difficult for everyone around you. You don't want that. No one wants that, but a lot do it anyway.

This is one of the main reasons why you need to build yourself a strong, honest and positive mindset. You need all the good things life has to offer, so you can make the right decisions. This is not hard work, it can be frustrating, but it is fun. When you get to the point that all the dots start to make sense, you constantly get better and better, in every way. Your whole life changes in the direction of the better, stronger, healthier (it's true, I didn't believe it either, but I love the bonus), wealthier and a friendlier you. I don't mean to say that you are none of these things, you are probably most of them, but they can always be better. Prepare to be surprised often. You will be. You see, when you have to deal with your passion, you want all the good things, because you understand how much better everything can be.

Don't let anyone convince you that it doesn't matter what you do. It does matter. What they usually mean is that you shouldn't be afraid to start with whatever you believe is right. There are so many just using the wrong wording for it. You learn a lot from it, skills, how much time you need, what you like to do, ways you like to work and last, but not least, you learn faster what your real passion is about. It's like targeting something you have never done before. You start by missing the essentials. You keep practicing and you get better. The more you practice, the smarter you work and the faster your progress will be. Then one day, you hit the target, you hit it again, and when you are really good, you barely manage to miss it. You know exactly what to do and you have a problem missing it. Practice and experience makes you better, smarter, more knowledgeable, stronger and secure.

Passion is a peculiar thing. It lets itself be hidden so you can experience a lot of other things. It plays "hide and seek" with you. You benefit from it, by getting stronger, learn lots of skills you can use to make your passionate work even better than you thought possible. It's fun, and yes, sometimes very frustrating. You will get to the point where you feel you are more than full of questions; you become a question mark yourself.

NOTHING CAN STOP YOU,
UNLESS YOU LET IT

"Problems are not stop signs, they are guidelines."

- Robert H. Schuller

You are responsible for your life. You may love it; a lot of people don't. Your life is exactly what you made it. When you read this, you have started to take responsibility for some changes you are looking for. Your passion may have hidden some parts you really would want to know. If you get annoyed or irritated, you have some fears about never finding it. Get rid of the fears; they don't serve you. All they do is make a kind of noise. They help you lose track of what you are searching for. Since everything happens for a reason, it would be of great help to find the reason. When you do, you will probably find what you were looking for in the first place.

When you take one step at a time and you know the reason for taking that step, there is a good chance you know what will come next. Here we have to get back to your planning for a moment. When you are taking your idea apart, you do it on the level you are, not the level you want to reach. Your plan would probably get more and more detailed and each of the details represent a task of some kind. Working smart would entail implementing those details in the plan. Find a natural place for it in your plan, and let it grow. The more details you have on your plan, the better and the smoother you get to the day of the results. Depending of the details in your plan, you can almost decide what will happen, and to get the strength you need, you should keep the end in mind.

Obstacles will occur. Even experienced marketers meet obstacles. They are also trying to learn something new. They are hopefully on another level, due to their experience.

Life passes by, whether you do something or not. Life happens all the time. We don't manage to plan everything to the details; too many people are involved, and it should not be necessary. The clue is to be as secure as possible, but you can't expect to have planned everything. You'd be out of challenges, in the end. (Don't worry, you will never be).

What if this happened:

While you were working on the project of your life, you had to spend some time to glue the pot that broke. You didn't really have time for it, but you had to do it now, for some reason. Suddenly you discover time had run very fast and you had to leave, without time to clean up, but you were a kind of happy, since you managed to finish the gluing. You rush out and do what you were supposed to do, get back home and you are met with an angry voice wishing you a loud "welcome home." The better half of your life was not happy at all, seeing the mess you left on the wrong table. It had been cleaned up, you are grateful, but you understand something is wrong. You had forgotten some friends were coming over while you were away. It had been planned a while ago, but since you knew you were away at the time they got there, you hadn't really bothered. If you apologize, you would more likely save the most of the evening, but if you started to yell back, Peace in the house would be the last thing to hope for in a while.

There was nothing deliberately done wrong in this situation; everyone had the best of intentions. Most people have the best of intentions all the time. The problem was this little detail of finishing what you started. When you start something, you should make sure you have the time for it, but sometimes you just don't. The way you handle the consequences makes the difference. If you don't take the responsibility for what you did <u>and</u> what you didn't do, if you try to find someone else to blame, you will notice that you easily get in trouble. Stand up for yourself, nicely, and if you can't complete it, make up for it in a way that helps to keep your eyes focused on your target.

When we are new to some kind of action, any action, we are not good at measuring time, but we take our chances. Sometimes we win: sometimes we learn something new. You only lose if you don't learn anything. Everything you learn will be of use sometime. If not today, maybe in a year; if not sooner, then later.

WHAT DO THINGS LOOK LIKE WHEN DOLLARS WANT YOU?

Excitement has its good sides and it can fool us. It's important that we keep track of the good sides and try to make them better. It's like building a road, first you make a path; then you see the direction; then you start to broaden the road as you keep wandering up and down. Then you make it look nice and repair the parts that fall below the standard you want. In the end, you've created a permanent road; you just use it naturally and you're proud of it, take care of it and keep it good looking.

The stronger your image is of what you want, the more curious the dollars get. They like people who take care of everything around them. Money likes to be respected as money, not as a slave. It likes to work and it likes to bring its friends back, to show them a nice place to be and a nice way of being treated. Money enjoys helping people, and when it does, their freedom makes it return to show you how well they did. You are, of course, grateful for its return and all the friends they bring. You have made a system that works fine for you and the money. When you keep building on what works, you understand what leverage really is about and how it works.

It all starts with a thought. You have a hunch about something, and you develop it into an idea. This idea is related to something you are good at, and you see a way to connect it to your passion. You decide to make a campaign, so you can spread the good idea to other people. The time flies and suddenly, it's all ready, just as planned. You do some calculations, find a reasonable price and you start your campaign. The moment you press enter, the campaign is on. It's a very exciting moment. Every detail works for you, and you know that where you announced your idea was the right place.

You have an idea of how the campaign will work because while you were preparing the campaign, you had the end in mind. The visualization of the results in your bank account has worked like a magnet for you. Your planning has been carefully adjusted through the whole process and you just know that what you do works. Keeping the result as visual as possible helps you to overcome any obstacle you meet. What you need to learn comes to you thanks to your awareness and your burning desire keep you going even when the going gets tough. You have successfully made a new campaign, you have learned a lot of new skills and you just did it. Time to reach those new goals, coming to you while working on the last one. You are grateful for all the opportunities coming to you and the dollars want to help you even more.

WHEN YOU'RE GRATEFUL AND SHOW IT, THIS HAPPENS

Gratitude is underestimated. What we take for granted, might be something we used to be grateful for. There are a lot of details that help us get through the day and for which we should be grateful. If you look around you, you will notice lots of details you have become so familiar with that you don't see the value they once had anymore. Gratitude is a way of reminding us of the fact that we have what we have. Not just material things; those closest to us, our family and friends, also need our gratitude. It doesn't matter if you have a good or bad relationship to your family and friends, you should be grateful for what you have and always want it to be better. You can do something; they can do something. Gratitude for what is good in your life will always be a good start.

Your passion, whether you know it or not, will manifest itself if you constantly show your trust in it. Your passion has always been with you, so you might want to pay a bit more attention to it, if you left it alone somewhere. Gratitude helps you keep on track when you're searching and it helps you keep it flowering when you find it. You create all the energy you need to make the most out of it, whatever it is. It would be a lot harder if we didn't have our passion. Being grateful for what you have and sharing it with other people is a great way of helping other people find their passion. The more you give, the more you get. How you get it is always a part of the mystery. Within it, lies a part of the enigma.

Next best steps!

1. *Write down, primarily in keywords, what you felt was most important for you, in this chapter. Save this list for six months, (schedule it in your calendar or make a reminder on your phone). When you open it, in six months, you might be surprised.*

2. *There are lots of tasks in this chapter. You should do them all, not just once, but again and again. Make a plan, test it, if it doesn't work, change the plan, don't give up. This is an exercise in testing, changing, test again and change what didn't work over and over again. Never give up. You'll be surprised in a short while, how much better you've become.*

Chapter 4

HOW TO MASTER A PROGRESSIVE SKILL SET

> *"The only place success comes before work is in the dictionary."*
> -   Lombardi

> *"Everything should be made as simple as possible, but not simpler."*
> -   Einstein

"How to make $3000 dollars a week in 30 days" - sounds too good to be true. It usually is. I didn't believe in this, so I joined a company. I wanted to prove it wouldn't happen. I was right, it didn't happen. It has happened for a handful of people, but it can only happen because you know what you are doing, you know where to find your customers and you know a way of marketing that works for the people you want to reach.

I learned all of that, but it took a lot longer than 30 days. I also found the inner game of some companies; their goal is to make themselves earn the $3000 dollars a week, out of the customers' pockets, including you. Later, if you're good, learn fast, work day and night, you can have the same advantage. Empty the pockets of other people, so they can sweat and maybe achieve some results, while paying a lot of money to someone else. That's the way I ended up seeing it; others had no problem with it, so they kept up their work. I didn't like what I had joined, I got out of it in time, but I spent my time well, observed how they worked, how people desperately tried to make their marketing work. Those who succeeded were always conscious of the importance of the mindset. They found a way to make Dollars Want Them.

My apologies if this offended someone. I just wanted to point out all the feelings that surface when you are unhappy with the results. The companies I joined are absolutely 'legit' companies. There is nothing wrong with what they do, but I wasn't ready for what I had to do. I didn't like the fact that a lot of others were in the same situation, so I decided to collect the information about what you need to learn before you join a company. I did my research on other companies as well, constantly finding more and better solutions on how to just collect the information without having to pay thousands of dollars for a service that didn't serve me. In addition, one of my goals was to find the solutions people were looking for, ones that could help start a business online from scratch and succeed.

The result of my research enabled me to do online marketing without spending more than necessary and knowing what information I needed to make a campaign successful. I also learned that even a good campaign can be unsuccessful. If people are not ready for what you offer, they won't buy into it. This is usually the result of targeting the wrong people, due to lack of proper testing. There is always that possibility, but as long as you do your best, you constantly get better. I made a summary of all my experiences, filtered out the bad feelings, got my feet on the ground and made a guide that wish to help you to success. You are reading it right now.

You should not expect results too fast, but as fast as possible. I've listened very carefully to a lot of webinars about making money fast. You always get the story of how fast they would have made it if they had the system they present. Later they tell you that they struggled for many years before they had their success. They tell the truth, but there is a twist. These people would make $3000 dollars a week in 30 days, because they know exactly what to do, where to find the customers, how to deal with the customers. They also have a lot of material to implement in their marketing, they have worked on their mindset and their marketing skills for years. In that position, everyone can make $3000 dollars a week.

There is also another catch in some of these programs. To make those dollars, they easily spend $2k dollars. Leaving them a profit of $1k. This only means that even if you earn a lot of money, you may need to spend a lot of money to feed the growth you want. It looks amazing when you see the amounts they earn, but it becomes quite ordinary when you see the end results.

Building a fortune takes time, no matter who you are. There is one rule that is more important than the others. It's not how much you earn, it's how much you keep. As long as you keep more than you spend, you will build a fortune. It will leverage. When you get more material to use, you can make more variations in your marketing, reach more people, increase your income and live a wealthy, healthy life in abundance.

"There are always two," as Master Yoda in Star Wars would have put it. He was talking about the dark forces, but this also applies to the good people. When someone works on making themselves more money, it's very often considered a bad thing. It isn't; the people are usually great and there is nothing wrong with the money. You use money, right? I believe you earn it and then you spend it. The question is the way you spend it. Is it to experience something or gain an advantage? In that case, I would call it an investment. You can use it to make more money. If you spend it for something you can't monetize, they are simply out of your system. Let's get back to these two people. They usually want you to succeed; unfortunately some are just not the teachers they want to be for some of their customers. There is just as much truth in the fact that some customers made a bad choice. We all do right and wrong, the best way of managing this is to start by admitting it. Successful online marketers never work alone. They usually don't talk much about it. They want you to take part in the community they have built, and that's great, you will meet interesting people and you can learn a lot. You should still keep looking for a partner who likes the way you work and vice versa. The importance of working together is the sharing of information, testing ideas, teaching each other what is needed in that situation, discussing the next step in a new project, when you need it and with someone you trust. Being a part of a community is great, but having someone closer may take your business to another level. There is no evil; it's just a fact that we all get better when we collaborate with someone sharing our way of working. These people succeed; so can you. Find your partner.

I didn't know anything about this when I started. I knew how to turn on the computer, surf the internet, chat with friends on social media and buy the stuff I was looking for. Most people can do that; these have become some of the most important functions of the Internet and probably the main way we use the Internet. The opposite side is where _you_ produce; _you_ give information, people search for what _you_ are making. It's very exciting and you should keep it in mind. Imagine when You are not the one searching for stuff on the Internet anymore; you are a creator of what people are searching for.

There is a difference in necessary actions when you are doing the marketing and when you are looking at the marketing. When you produce your material, you want people to find it, enter your site and take the actions you want them to take. By keeping it simple, you will see this happen more often than if you make a complex website. Many marketers lose their customers because the process of ordering the products is too complicated. They give up, find another site offering something similar with easier access to the product. This is what you want to avoid. Make it simple, but not simpler.

Your skills will automatically improve when you use them. The more often, the better you get. The better you get, the more you get done within the timeframe you have set. When you have a partner, you are more likely to reach your goals in time. It's very interesting to see how embarrassing it gets when you don't keep your promises.

YOU HAVE AN IDEA

"An idea, like a ghost, must be spoken to a little before it will explain itself "

- Charles Dickens

Your ideas are serious, no matter how weird they may seem. Consider them a gift. I know some people say they never get any ideas, and they are usually right. Did you know that you can change that? Even if you never had an idea in your life, you can come up with them. You already do, but you somehow suppress them. You can start by saying: "I am serious about all my good ideas," several times, every day. Yes, it sounds weird, I know, but it works. If it works, you should do it. It's not about believing, it's about knowing. This happens. You tell yourself that you have ideas, they are good and you want to do something about them, even if you never tried before; this will happen. You are waking up that part of you, the part that constantly looks for new opportunities.

When you have your idea, make it grow while you start taking the actions needed to make it a reality. As we let the seed of a plant grow in the soil, we need to let our ideas grow in our brain. The idea will require some attention, of course; you need to really learn to know it, so you can make the best of it. This is done by working on it, making the product or the marketing campaign. This is nurturing the idea and as you move along, it gets better, stronger and more solid. Just like a seed, you trust it to be where it is, the seed in the soil and the idea in the brain. Don't disturb it. Create it and picture how great it will be when you have finished the work. Always keep an eye on the end result.

MAKE THE IDEA SIMPLE

Everything can be made simpler. You just take it apart. Just like a mechanic takes apart a car, you can take apart ideas. It gets easier to realize your idea. Enter each of the parts in your plan instead of just entering the idea.

Let me explain. When you have a great idea for a product, let's say you want to create an e-book about making a wooden terrace. The book is meant to be for those who are trying to build their own terrace, so it should be detailed. You want to make sure that as many as possible get all the points. If you know everything, you just write it down, but if you need to check out some details, do the necessary research, one by one, and save the results in one folder on your computer. Maybe you want to use some pictures or drawings of the process, then you have to either search for them, take the pictures yourself or maybe you want someone else to do it for you. If you are good at drawing, you do it yourself, if not, you buy the service from someone who gladly does it for you. When you have made all the research, and collected all the pieces you want to use, you start assembling the e-book. Carefully and in a friendly tone, you explain everything with all the details necessary. You divide the e-book into chapters, make the headings and create a cover. This is the process of taking an idea apart and assembling it. You have made your idea into a product. You can sell it or give it away.

This is the same process I used when I was building my wooden terrace. I knew what it would look like when it was finished, so all I had to do was to "take it apart", in my mind. The first thing I noted was the deck. I had to find out how much material I needed. The deck would need solid material underneath, so all in all, I needed several different sizes of lumber. Since I didn't have too much knowledge about the sizes normally used, I had to do some research on what measures the lumber dealer had to offer. Research doesn't have to be so difficult, it just has to be done. There was some digging that needed to be done to make the terrace stable. I had to search to find the material that would help me get a good result. The screws, nails and tools had to be checked to avoid surprises when I built it. When I had my list of details, I collected what I had and bought what I needed. When everything was where it was supposed to be, all I had to do was make the wooden terrace. My solution, created in my mind, had become a reality. It works very well and does exactly what I wanted it to do. It makes my gardening easier and it is a wonderful place to relax in the sun.

The more often you take apart your ideas, the easier it gets and the more details you will find. You will find some details you can act on right away, some you need to study, learn more about and along the road, you will find details you want to study because they look interesting. (At any rate, you can always use them later). Take care of the details when you assemble the parts and you will make great products.

What do you know already about how to realize your idea? The answer to the question is where you start. Always start with what you know. Every finished part is finished, waiting for the rest. The more parts that are finished, the more inspiration you give yourself.

Learning something new should be on your daily task list. One thing at a time, but always learning something new. While you learn, make sure you practice it. The best part of the practice is when you immediately can use it on something you want to promote in your marketing. In addition to learning something new, you get into the habit of making it profitable, you get the spark to get the work done, and you get the good feeling you need to make the marketing great.

Parts it will take you too long to learn are best left to someone who knows what he or she is doing. There is always someone offering their services to help you. The costs are usually low, depending on the workload. The search for help will even make you learn something new, so it is a win-win situation. You get the parts done; some new knowledge and other people can help you for a decent charge. If you can't leave it to someone else, you just have to do it yourself, remember to add the time you need into your plan. A lot of great ideas have ended in the drawer, because the creator never managed to finish them. A finished product is of more use than a never finished perfect product. Take away the pride, grow into the habit of finishing and then get proud of what you finished. You can always polish it later. This is called upgrading or improving and gives you a great opportunity for another campaign. The more campaigns, the more customers.

MULTIPLYING THE IDEA

Your product, the finished result should be multiplied. If it is a physical item, you need to contact someone who can help you to produce it, unless you can do it yourself. Digital products are usually made once and then offered as downloadable copies. This can be done in many ways, no solution is better than the other, but knowing about as many as possible makes it easier to find what suits your product. Every product of any kind can be upgraded or improved. If you make your products keep up with the Joneses, (not you, just your products), a few hours' work now and then can make you a real success for a long time.

While you are working on the details, you will see other solutions that will in turn lead to yet other new ideas. One idea is always the starting point for other ideas. Don't mix the new ideas with the one you are working on. Make the necessary notes, just enough to get back to that moment and start working on the new idea after you finish what you are working on. Make it a habit to finish one thing at a time; it will save you a lot of frustration.

WHO WANTS THIS?

When you get your ideas, make sure you target the right people with the right purpose. Keep asking yourself; Who are the people who want this, and how does it help them? What are the reasons why they want this help? Ask the questions while you work on it; take notes as keywords on a separate piece of paper. This is golden information when you are ready to create your marketing campaign.

The next step is to find where these people meet each other. They are connected somewhere. Find their connection platform and start communicating with them. Don't try to sell your product before you know how to speak to them. Communication is what keeps people together; it is also what keep people getting away from others when used wrongly. I still believe you are more likely to revisit a shop with friendly, helpful, informative employees than someone pushy, loud, never-stop-talking, stressful employees. Communication is the key to get in touch with people; it is also what makes us keep together, when used correctly.

MAKE YOUR PLAN

If you don't have a plan, you easily get lost in the process. It is very confusing and is a part of the "preparing to fail" paradigm. Online marketing is simple, just not easy. To make it easier, it's important that you keep track of what you have to do and make a natural order of doing it. The next step is to track your work, see how people respond and do the necessary adjustments.

When you get the experience, you will naturally develop your plan while you work. If this is the first time you are going to make an online campaign, you should take some time just to make the plan. This will give you invaluable insight on how you work and what you need to improve.

"Insanity is doing the same thing over and over again and expecting different results."

- Albert Einstein

When you get your idea, the smart way of starting your planning is right away. As you take notes on the parts you need to make, to learn, which ones to outsource, make a space for the when. It's not always easy to set a date, but set them in the order you feel is right.. If you have to change it later, change it. The point is to stick to the plan, make everything happen in the right order and know that you are on your way. Always try to stipulate when the whole project should be finished. Even if it's tomorrow, always make that plan. You can use it again and again and again. It doesn't have to be the same each time, you change what you need to change, but you end up having a template that will help you work a lot faster.

Every part of your idea should be taken care of. Enter them in your plan, big or small; it doesn't matter. If you have them in your plan, save them in your "library"; you can always (for instance ten years from now) get back to it and you will say, "yeah, that's how we do that".

YOUR MARKETING PLAN – THE STEPS YOU TAKE

A marketing plan is a part of the major plan for the product. It says something about where you do your marketing, how you do your marketing, who it is for and what marketing tools you want to use.

Your product is what you want them to buy into, whether it is some free information you want to spread or it is an item you want them to pay for. People are people and they communicate in a certain way. If you want to reach them, you need to consider a few things. Is this product for other products you have made, or is there a need for a separate website for this product? Very often, you can use a site you have made before; you just make new pages for the product and use those links in your marketing. Search engines love sites that change and develop, so as you expand a website, there is a greater chance that people will find it by searching for it. Mainly, you will need to direct people to your site and have their visit be a part of the ranking of your site. The more visitors, the better rank (usually, but there is no fixed rule about this).

The major step to make sure it works is how you deal with the magical 5 seconds. When you make your marketing plan, you should consider what it is on your site that makes people want to stay there for more than 5 seconds. If you don't succeed, you can always try something else later. Start with what you believe in, test it and work it into success as you get more and more skilled and experienced. Never let a beginning stop you from beginning. There will always be a second, third, fourth chance. When you have done this a few times, you understand what to do.

EFFICIENCY OF SIMPLICITY

There is a quote that has meant a lot to me in the process of becoming who I am:

> *"Perfection is achieved,*
> *not when there is nothing more to add,*
> *but when there is nothing left to take away."*
> \- Antoine de Saint-Exupery

When we start something new, we want everything in there. We easily over-complicate everything. In the end, it gets more confusing and complicated than rocket science. The one obstacle is replaced by another and we lose track of what we started.

Learning to make things simpler, just keeping what has to be there and then carefully adding what we want is a much better approach. When you see a site with a thousand items, don't lead yourself to believe it's how it started. Every site started with something simple, evolving into whatever it has become. There are, of course, the exceptions. Large companies hire companies to produce their websites using people who do it for a living. This is not where you want to start, (unless you have a huge company or a special addiction to outsourcing everything to others, that is). Simplicity and the love of what a site is for, not how it looks, makes your project come along a lot faster than if you spend all your time making it look good. It's not the appearance that makes the site, it's the content. The easier it is to find exactly what you want to find, perform the actions you want them to take, the more customers or visitors you get. They will stay there and probably visit again, because your site made it easy for them to do exactly what you wanted them to. People like to spend as little time as possible on a site, but not less.

THE PEOPLE

One rule applies to everything you do:

Some people like what you do.
Some people don't like what you do.

There is a balance. You will never be able to please everyone. Never try to. Decide who you are speaking to in your marketing BEFORE you start writing the content. If you don't know who you are speaking to, no one will listen. It's like talking to yourself in a street full of people. They have other interests and keep moving, (until you address them specifically). All your efforts in making your product and your campaign will be in vain. Your great qualities will not be shown and it makes everyone lose. You lose your well earned attention and someone out there has to keep looking for what they want, but never finds it. You wouldn't start talking about knitting in an audience of snooker enthusiasts, would you?

WHERE AND WHEN YOU ADVERTISE MATTERS

There are many ways of spreading the good word of your mission. When you are new to online marketing, it may seem a bit confusing. This has mainly to do with the fact that you are performing actions you are not used to. Everything feels a bit weird when it's new, but as you get into the habit of believing in what you do, knowing the potential of what you are marketing, you will discover that you are the expert. Your control of your mindset is of invaluable help to make the right decisions and perform your marketing in a trustworthy manner.

Another thing about being new to online marketing is how well your audience knows you. It's like a band having a concert. You want as many people as possible to know about you and what you do. You want them to like you and you want them to take the right actions. It all begins with you knowing where the right people are. This does sometimes take a while, but the smartest way of starting is to search all the social media you are familiar with. Learn how you communicate naturally with the people. When you have your product ready, you mention it, lead them to your website and if they are hooked, you have a customer.

You want them to be on your list. A list is, as mentioned in chapter 2, one of the cheapest ways of marketing. Your effort pays off again and again, without you having to pay anything. There are marketers calling their list the private ATM machine. It is recommended to take care of your customers, to make sure they get the offers they want, without being spammy.

When you know who your audience is, it is easier to set up an advertisement. Advertising on social media doesn't have to be expensive, and done the right way (according to what product you have), it can be very successful. A lot of beginner marketers believe that the customers just pour in, like a heavy rainshower. I'm sorry to say that this is a myth. When you are well known for what you do, it can happen, but usually not in the beginning. Imagine yourself, when you see something you are interested in advertised on the social media you use. Do you believe everyone is someone you can trust? Most of us don't, it's human to hesitate a bit, get to know the person and then check it out. Still, advertising is very effective, and when done the right way, you will succeed, as long as you never stop.

Knowing your product is essential. If you don't, would you buy from yourself? Trust is also important, especially when it comes to online marketing and what you do. If you own the product you are selling and keep telling how and when you use it, people are more likely to follow you. One essential rule is that people do what you do, not what you say. (The best test of this is children. Tell them to do something; if you're lucky, it works. Show them how to do it, and the success rate skyrockets. Grownups work the same way).

Some products are seasonable; if yours are, make sure your potential customers know you well ahead of the season. This is to make sure they want to purchase your product, since they trust you, when you present it. Trust is built over time, not in an instant.

Focus on the parts of your marketing that work. Don't try to do everything at once. When you find a solution that works for you, keep using it, get better at it and enjoy the success. At the same time, it is important to test new areas. You know the famous cage? The one we all are inside, you may have heard the story of the bear who had been locked inside a cage all his life. It was decided to let the bear out, to let it have its freedom. They opened the door, the bear sat in the cage, looking out, studying the difference. After a while, he crept closer to the opening, stuck his head out, pulled it back and then remained inside the cage. Some time later, he tried again, this time going all the way out, but staying close to the cage. It doesn't lose sight of it, and then, suddenly, he went back inside. "Safety," prevented him from seeing freedom. We have a lot of the same. We keep doing what we are used to do, not because we like it, but we feel safe. This safety is false. The worst examples are the people who don't dare leave their house. They don't know what it's like out there. Television news tells them it's dangerous, so they will not leave their house. They are trapped in their own home; their freedom to do whatever they like has been taken away from them.

Taking the step outside of the cage, leaving the cage and never going back is what freedom is about. The freedom to do whatever you want is a clear target objective when you are working on getting your well earned Lifestyle instead of a regular living.

Do something you have never done before – this is a very good practice to reach this target. If you are new to online marketing, have little or no contact with people on social media, now is a good time to start practicing. Any social media you have heard of are of interest. You should start by making your communication conversational; continue by learning how to make friends (not best friends, but friendly enough to make them buy what you have to offer). The last step is to build a good relationship with you as the provider of products that they are happy to buy.

Always have a new target on what should be the next social media or the next thing you should be familiar with.

Your advertising along with your presence is what makes you successful. The more you work on it, the better you get, the more fun it is, the more customers you get. This is a great way to start your success slowly and grow as you build your business. Always take notes. They come in handy when you start testing new areas where you might find more customers. You are very likely to find good friends as well, along with a lot of marketers. Don't let anything surprise you, but never forget your mission.

YOUR TIME - YOUR RESPONSIBILITY

*"Everywhere is within walking distance
if you have the time."*
- Steven Wright

Every one of us have 24 hours a day. No more, no less.
We are responsible for how this time should be
apportioned. An old ideal was to work 8 hours, sleep 8
hours and spend the last 8 hours with your friends and
family. This was before we got television, mobile phones,
tablets and computers. Everything became so very
efficient, especially after we got the computers, that we
lost the time we had left. The world works in mysterious
ways, but we can solve the mysteries.

People sit in front of their computer 8 hours a day at
work, get home and spend 4-6 hours in front of the TV
while surfing on the phone, the tablet or playing games,
then spending the rest of the evening to check e-mail, the
weather, social media, games, news and more on the
tablet, the phone or the computer. Is this a life well lived?

More and more people are having problems sleeping;
they don't feel they are connected with their family, and
everyone wonders why. Prioritizing the important things
in life is the answer. Some things are just more important
than others. Everyone succeeding online (and elsewhere),
knows this. What are your priorities?

You know what time you have and you can do something
about it. It's not recommended to change a winning sleep
pattern. It doesn't help, it makes things worse. The time
you have sold to your employer is not an option, so for

most beginners, there are about 8 hours you can change to create your online marketing. Make the time you need by changing the way you spend your time. Use the time you have efficiently, do what you have to do, take away all possible distractions, never gamble on multitasking (scientifically proven again and again that we are not made for it. The debate is still going on, but what you will experience is that you will learn a lot more by doing one thing at a time. Be present in the moment and you will get the workload flow faster, you will also notice that you get more and more done, because you like it and you are improving your skills).

The amount of time you have available should always increase a little one month later. It's like hunting for treasures. Finding ways of doing what you have to do in less time than you usually do. Never stop the search for more time you can free up. There are tons of books about how to do this, and everyone can give you great tips on how to free your time in the preparation for your new Lifestyle. Keep the end in sight. Imagine yourself living the lifestyle you want and before you know it, you get the feeling of being there. That moment is the beginning of your new Lifestyle.

Let every part of your plan respectively take the time it takes, but not more. In the beginning, it can be a bit hard to reach all your goals on time. Adjust the plan. Never leave your tasks undone (well, that is technically not possible, but sometimes you get that feeling, simply because you know you could have done them better). Some tasks have to be improved later, but usually, when you focus on one thing at a time, you will be amazed by what you are capable of. The only limit on what you can do is your lack of belief in what you can do. Change that and you will smile your way through what people call trouble but you now call challenges. Never limit your challenges, Challenge your limits and you'll be fine.

Keep an eye on how much time everything takes. Don't stare at your watch, but try to estimate it, set an alarm and then set a goal to finish before the alarm goes crazy and buzzes. It's always a great victory to beat the alarm.

Do one thing at a time. Take full responsibility for yourself. Yes, I'm aware of the repetition here. I already mentioned it. I'll say it again: Do One Thing At A Time. Do not underestimate the importance. In a year or so, you will be grateful for taking that responsibility.

Keep track of your work. Keep a diary, preferably a notebook, where it is easy to take notes, just a few keywords here and there. They will also serve you when you are looking for keywords for your website.

If you learn something where you need to make more notes, you might want to make a document to save on your computer. Create a Folder, which is easy to find, calling it My Library can be a good idea (*it helped me a lot, and now when I have located most of the documents I have produced with vital information, I just pop into the library, search for the keywords and easily find what I need. Absolutely recommended. Keep the keyword in the title of the documents when you save it in the library. Hours are saved. You can use the hours for your marketing or practice your new lifestyle.*)

YOUR PROGRESS DEPENDS ON YOUR SKILLS

"Start by doing what's necessary;
then do what's possible;
and suddenly
you are doing the impossible."
- Francis of Assisi

Decide when you will learn the new skills you need. When you have a plan, you can spare yourself a lot of stress by scheduling when you need to learn your new skills. At first it takes some time to learn something new, but you even learn to be more efficient in your learning when you are constantly aware that you are learning something new.

The best way of learning it, is by using it. You may need to spend a bit more time than what you've planned, but you learn two things. You can always change your plan and you can always attempt to make it happen according to the plan. You learn about your planning and you use it as a tool, not a product. The difference is that a tool needs to be adjusted to fit what it's supposed to fix, but a product should be as finished as it possibly can be. If you want to change it later, you can, but why not use the experience to create a better one? Just a suggestion.

When you learn something new, you do yourself a great favor by taking notes. If you strive to make it like a recipe (or a manual, if you want), you will thank yourself later. Recipes are easily dug into again and again, you get the information you need very fast, and it is of great help for your progress in your work. You don't have to stop for hours to find out how on earth you did it. That is a waste of time, and we don't like that, do we?

This new skill might be needed later. Some are rarely in use, while others are used all the time. You will change the ones that are much used, depending on how you do your marketing. When you see some changes in the market, you may find the need for some skills you haven't used in a while. These moments are best served with your making of manuals (the recipes). When you use those manuals again, you may want to make them better. Don't spend the time perfecting them the first time; you make the notes you believe are necessary and then you improve it next time. In this way, you teach yourself a great way to improve your work and you become more and more aware of the details.

In some cases, it will be natural to make templates. When you have a set of products you want to look similar, you should start by making a template. Decide what colors to use, what kind of pictures, what fonts to be used and every detail you feel should be taken care of. If you have a problem with it, don't be shy. Ask someone. If you know someone who is good at what you need, discuss it. Another solution, of course, is to buy the service from someone else. There is always a website with the service you need. In the end, you might be the expert; you know best, no one else. If you have found your partner, these are all great topics.

When you have your templates and your manuals, you can easily share them as a part of your service; you might even find a way to profit from it. Everything you do is of value, and everything of value is needed by someone. What you share might be someone else's salvation.

Sharing, the right way, will benefit you. Just make sure you do what feels right.

6 STEPS ON YOUR WAY TO SUCCESS

1. **The Way You Market Yourself Is The Way You Get Response.** *You must believe in what you market. The way you market it, gives you the response you deserve. Deserve? Yes, maybe it's not the response you wanted, but you get the response you deserve depending on your marketing. If you believe in what you do, but don't get any response, you need to make some changes. You have what you have because of what you did. If you want something else, DO something else. Make sure that you direct your marketing towards the people you want to reach. By making the plan, you are able to turn your marketing into a success. As long as you know how to find your way of doing just that.*

2. **Your products must be of a quality that people want.** *Whatever you want to sell, there are people who want it. In other words, everything can be marketed. You want your customers to be satisfied, don't you? Affiliating any kind of product may work, but the better the quality, the larger the success. If you have your own products, make sure your customers are satisfied by providing quality. Quality always makes people come back.*

3. **Having a list of customers is a wise thing.** *Now you know that you have found your audience and your products are wonderful. Great job, so far. When you believe in your products, your customers are more likely to buy more from you again and again. By making a customer list, you can send them more offers and keeping them informed on important matters of your business, your customers won't forget you. You give the offer and when your returning customers see the offer (usually in an e-mail) and they see it is from you, they are more likely to buy from you. Why? You built your trust on your blog/website and since you deliver the goods and they are great, they know they can trust you.*

4. **Time-saving options.** *There are many ways of saving time. Without any shortcuts on the actions you need to take, you would start early in the morning and still be up late at night. Exhausted. Being exhausted does not help your success. You make more mistakes and you don't get the good ideas on how to market yourself. That is why you need to know what can help you. There are many ways of doing that, but a good way to start is to listen to experienced people who don't tell you because they want to sell you something, but because they know it works. Make a plan on how much time you can spend and what you do in that time. If not, you'll be sitting around doing a lot for nothing, spending all the time in the world. That's not worthwhile.*

5. **You should look for a partner, a mentor or a group of people with experience to talk to.** *A partner and a mentor (or a mastermind group) wants you to succeed, and they'd love to help you out. Experienced people with the answers to all your questions are a great help.*

6. **Make sure you know how to sell and market your product.** *If you don't know how to sell, you need to learn something about it. You never stop learning, so age is not an excuse. The only excuse is a lack of interest in an online marketing success. Anyway, it is always a good idea to know how to sell and how to market. You never know when you'll need it.*

Next best steps!

In the previous chapter, you might have gotten an idea about how online marketing can serve you. Test your skills in mastering a progressive skill set by using the keywords you wrote down in chapter 3. Try to make your marketing plan, based on one of those keywords (or maybe you have found some new ones? Your choice). Play around with it, what do you need to learn now to implement your new planning skills?

Chapter 5

HOW TO OVERCOME OBSTACLES THAT PREVENT SUCCESS

"You wake up, rise and do your morning routines passionately. You can't wait to get into action. The plan you perfected last night just propels you through the routines. You are determined to make every detail of the plan a reality. Today. You have all the time you need, you know you can do all the technical details like clockwork and control all the practical and social issues in your llife. Your plan eliminated all the obstacles you could possibly be aware of. You are a success. You can do absolutely everything you need or want to do and you reach any goal you set."

That's a great life in a nutshell. If you have a problem getting into the nutshell, crack it open and let the good life come to you. This is living a lifestyle, and you are the creator of it by taking the right actions.

Your time, your technical skills and your social connections, including all the practical issues that follow, play a major role in preventing you from success. When you think to yourself, "I don't have time for this", start adding Yet to that sentence. When you hear your voice say "I don't know how to do this", add a strong Yet to it and if you hear that inner voice tell you "I can't communicate with those strangers", keep adding the Yet. The word Yet neutralizes the sentence and gives you the direction you need to turn despair into faith. It also implies that you will have the time, you will know how to do it and you will know how to communicate with strangers. You already do, you are just not used to it, Yet.

"Obstacles are those frightful things you see when you take your eyes off your goal."

\- Henry Ford

THE TIME YOU HAVE

For years, I've been telling myself, "When I get time, I will....". The rest of the sentence has been about different interests or actions, but I've had a few recurring ones. They seem to follow me everywhere I go. Time, on the other hand, never did, until I learned the difference between "when I get the time" and "when I take the time." When was the last time someone gave you time, as a gift? It never happens. They might have said, "take your time," but at the same time they have told you what you should do while you "take your time".

We are in a way stuck with our 24 hours a day and how we use it depends on our personal choices. You can choose to let others decide for you, which is exactly what has happened when you say: "I need to go to work." Actually, you don't need to go to work. You choose to go to work. It's a commitment you gave your employer, you turn up at work and your employer pays you for the time you work. You sold your time to your employer. I hope you like what you do. A study shows that 70% of all employees do not like what they do.

If you love what you do, you use time wisely; you do what you're supposed to do, and suddenly it's time to go to bed. You don't even get tired that easily. You are in a good mood and you enjoy most of your minutes while you are doing what you do. This is time well spent and makes you look forward to the next day, when you can continue or start something new, full of excitement and ready to reach that goal, set new goals, and smile.

The way you use your time is the way you have chosen to use it. I frequently hear "I had to ... even though I didn't like it," in school, when the pupils are forced to take some kind of action to learn something new or something they don't feel comfortable with. They are more likely to blame someone else rather than themselves. In a way they are right, but sometimes we have to do something to move on. There are many pupils who do not see the point of learning what they have to learn, which makes them insecure, skeptical and less motivated. The teacher is a kind of mentor for them, a guide who leads them to the next level in that particular subject, but so many of the pupils don't understand it this way, they are more concerned about when the class ends than what they can learn. Sometimes this leads to a situation where the pupils blame the teachers for making them do things they don't want to do, still believing they don't need it. The truth is, of course, that they don't know what they need, or what they might need it for. This makes the days in school very tense. The pupils don't understand the meaning of what they are learning and the teachers are looked upon as slave drivers. Of course this is an extreme version of everyday life at school, but it's still reality for some. All of these good people, both pupils and teachers, are kept in the system to make sure that everyone grows up knowing how to make a living. By learning what everybody needs to know, everybody can make a living. They are able to get a job, get a family, get a house and a car, act properly according to the culture you live in. They do what the others are doing and give everyone the opportunity to feel just fine. Everything else is up to each and everyone as individuals.

People are creatures of habit. This is good and bad news. Let's take a quick look at a few of the topics. The habits you learn in school enable you to make a living. Making a living entails letting your new habits enable you to make money. Making money makes you want more. Having more enables you to spend more money; you do what you are used to, so you work more to make more money. You do what other people do when you need even more money; you look for a better paid job. You may have to work more, but you get a better salary. This money is used to pay all the new bills, make the house look even better, get a new car, more expensive vacations and so on. You are deep into the system of ordinary habits and there is a big chance you will get lost somewhere along the way.

We are not actually made for making a living; we are made to live. Public expenses make it necessary to ensure that everyone gets the knowledge they need

[139]

simultaneously, which of course is very difficult. If we were equal in all ways possible, it might have worked better, but no matter how you look at it, it is very complicated to make such a huge system work properly for everyone. The solution is that everyone needs to learn everything and get an idea of what they should do as a minimum. This prepares everyone to get a job and make a living, but not very much more than that. What is good about it, for everyone, is that you learn to work habitually. You understand the point of learning, reading, listening, taking notes and debating or at least talking about the subject. The point being continuously. The more often you receive input from what you are learning, the better you get at it and the sooner you make a habit of it. When you understand this, you can use it for whatever you need to learn to turn your life into Your Life.

You can turn your habits into what you want. Imagine your day once you have succeeded. Your planning is constantly getting better and better. You have built your platform and on top of it you have placed your burning desires. Let's use a house as an example. After you build the platform, you sketched the house, (got the help you needed), you built the house (still with the help you needed) and then you started your new life in the house. What a great feeling. This is what you want.

When you get there, you will also notice that you are wanted. What you do is an inspiration for other people. Maybe you don't want the house, but build your online marketing business. The principles are the same. You believe in it, you collect all the information you need, you produce all the products you need (everything with the help you need), you create your business and use all your skills to run it. When you find you need a new skill, you learn it while you use it, so it's implemented as a part of what you do, faster. When you do this passionately, often enough, you make it a habit to perform all the tasks needed, and you have even more to celebrate when you succeed.

Understanding and constantly reminding yourself of the fact that you don't want a living, you want a lifestyle, heightens your interest in finding the time to start building your platform. Find time? No, I'm sorry; life goes by if you don't take action on it. You have to make and take your time. You need your time to make more time, and then you spend that time building your new life. Now is always a good time to start.

Time is your number one asset; you want to control it.

YOUR NUMBER ONE ASSET

"I'd rather an imperfect now, than a perfect never!"
• Unknown

Time is the most precious thing you have. Every second goes by and disappears. You will never have that second again. How you spend your time is what makes your day and how you spend your days makes up your weeks, months and years. The more present you are in the moment, the more you will experience and the more you will do to make your life Your Life. If you don't take part in the moment, you will never be a part of it. That moment is gone; it has left the building and will never return.

"I can always do it another day", is a very popular statement. It's also one of the great reasons why people never get to the successful part of life. When all you do is what you should have done some time ago, you never get the "flow" and the good feeling that enables you to say, "that's it. Now I can do something else or maybe just have fun," without the struggle. If you constantly have a bad conscience about all the tasks you should have done, you have a hard time enjoying what you do. This has to do with making enough time to do what you are supposed to do, that is, lay a good plan, work through the tasks at the time (or just day) you were supposed to do them, and stick to the plan until you have reached your goals. I need to mention that plans are changeable. If you find your plan too optimistic, it is better to expand it a little. This will create the space you need to be flexible. This is also an important action to take, to make sure you get to your goals instead of just achieving them only halfway and never managing to continue.

There is a time for everything, and when you understand the signals and do what they tell you to do, you will experience a completely different lifestyle. I was completely stuck in doing everything for everyone all the time. When I sat down to do what I had planned (sometimes planned way ahead), I was exhausted. Sitting as if paralyzed, doing what I really, really wanted to do, completely without the ability to enjoy it, made it very difficult to continue and finish. It always ended up with a very good start and then a steep downhill slide into the sand, buried deep down like something that "wasn't meant to be". My problem was "lack of time", (of course it wasn't, that's just what I told myself) coupled with a very optimistic plan. I used to plan as if I didn't have anything else to do in the whole world. You get very exhausted if your plan is too tight. You have feelings of guilt and low self-esteem. You don't need the guilt, but you do need to believe that YOU can do it. There is no question about the fact that you can, but somehow you get so full of all the doubts possible (and maybe then some...) that it does not seem to be worth it. Schedule the time you need to fulfill your tasks, and be rational, but not too rational. Make it a challenge, but not too challenging. Adjust your plans and expect to be better at what you do. When you get better, you work faster. Make yourself the challenge, by incorporating the need to work faster in your plan. You will feel the competition. Nothing is better than competing with yourself, even if you lose, you win.

Making good plans isn't enough, you would also create a huge advantage for yourself if you made a list (at least) of all the obstacles that could occur. Everything that could possibly disturb you should be included. Yes, that too, whatever you were thinking of, and make sure that everyone knows that when you work, you work. Time to do the work is recognized by the restlessness in the body. It's a signal for you to take action by closing the door, shutting down everything that can disturb you, even the phone. Focus on what you are going to do, according to your plan (preferably) and stop when you planned to. When you're focused, you don't want to be contacted by others. You want to finish what you started.

How about all these things that were not "meant to be" – are they gone forever?

Maybe some of them were not meant to be, but others keep turning up, at least for me, and since I'm just a regular human, I believe that is what happens to others as well. Some of my ideas, were nicely presented by other people who also got the idea. Fair enough. What I didn't do, someone else got, took action on it and turned into success. Should I be angry or jealous? Of course not. I had the chance, but didn't act on it. My bad.

Some things keep turning up, in my case they have been around since childhood, so it's obvious to me that I should make them a reality. They are huge, and I am working on them now, but they take time and I love to spend time making them a reality. Doing that is living a lifestyle. I hope that you have one or more of those "yeah, I know the feeling, it's like I just have to do it," - moments. We are all talented and meant to do something, and usually both at the same time. Now is always a good time to act on it.

As you get better at your skills and your planning starts to work more regularly, you will be thrilled by the time you save. This is a great time to keep making new plans for what you are going to do next, what you want to make or sell. Make the list, include what you need to learn and you are on your way to make it a smooth and enjoyable ride. Keep the smile on your face by knowing that you will succeed. Maybe you need to adjust your plans every now and then, but perfect it for the next day before you go to bed and you will wake up with a big smile on your face the next morning.

You want to avoid my journey, so here is what you don't want:

I had this great idea, learned what I needed and how to do it. I kept going on, great stuff, some fun days, then some troublesome times, but got through the obstacles, then a bit slower, frequently not having the time to sit *down or being tired and then all the other things came along. There was always something else I had to do. I had to change my plan, forgot a few details, started over again and then I was a bit tired, but ready to go. A few days passed, and then, when I sat down to continue... nothing happened. No strength, no good solutions, only the desire to finish, but completely out of fuel, and down we go. Again and again and again. In the end I stopped trying. My fire died out. It got very difficult to get up in the morning, just to get back to the regular life I had. Again and again and again... especially when <u>you still want to pursue your goal</u>, but can no longer see how this could even happen. Did you ever say to yourself, "It's just a dream....."?*

Commit yourself to make sure your dreams are reality. When do you want them to become real?

> **<u>Do this now:</u>** *write down a rough timetable of your days. Make columns if you wish. One for each of the seven days. Include everything that occurs regularly. You need this for your complete plan.*

I hope I didn't scare you with my story above. Without knowing the reality of time, you can easily despair, so you should do the little exercise above before you continue.

WHEN TO WORK?

Look at the weekly schedule you just drew up. Some people get scared when they do this, but there's no need to. You've made it so far in life, so why not take it one step further?

When would be a good time to schedule a couple hours during which you wouldn't be interrupted? People are creatures of habit, meaning: so are you. This is a simple and great way of developing that new habit you want to acquire. If you can find the same time every day, you should use that time. Start with an hour, preferably two hours, but at least one. It's like starting something new. You cannot learn everything at once. Begin slow and increase the tempo and amount of time as you get better at it. If you try to do everything at once, you are preparing to fail, not to succeed.

There is an important reason for not spending all the time you have. There is more than one reason, actually, but here we are talking about the fact that you have to "study". There is no need to be afraid, it's only about reading, listening to audios, looking at videos and study what other people do, how to do it and then test yourself and get it into your plan. This takes time as well, especially in the beginning. At the same time it is a very good habit to get into. You learn a lot about what this is all about. You learn a lot by studying the work of other people, and everyone else does it, there's nothing wrong in doing it, on the contrary, it's more fun. You spend less time learning and get more time to spend on other things.

Another important reason is getting into the habit of focusing on one thing at a time. When you work you work, when you study, you study.

A third important reason is that you don't want to be burnt out during your first month. When your new habits are a part of your daily practice, you already focus on work and you study separately. After a short while, you will find it natural to use what you've read, listened to and watched simultaneously, like training. You learn by doing what you read, hear and see.

A platform works best when all the parts are equally strong. Time management is a part of your platform. There is a bonus in doing it this way, you will discover it, and it's amazing.

> **_Do this now:_** *decide how many hours you can work on your new lifestyle, make at least a rough estimate and start with one or preferably two hours per day. Spend a few minutes to write it down, now.*
> *(You will naturally want to increase the number of hours as you get the hang of the work you need to do. You will find a way to take more of your time for this work. Always remember to start slow and take it up a level at a time. Keep challenging yourself, but make sure you have enough time to sleep and make the next day a beautiful one. It's like a plane; stop on the runway, increase speed, lift off, enjoy the flight and land at your destination and smile.)*

Time to take action!

WHEN TO HAVE FUN?

Now, is always a good time to have fun.

The reward of scheduling your time for work properly is that you can have fun without a bad conscience. You know your platform is coming along and after working at the scheduled time, you can relax, feel the comfort of taking actions for your new life and suddenly it's time to have some fun.

As you go along your new path, you will have fun when doing the work. If you constantly appreciate your new skills and your new knowledge, you will have fun. Humans are made for new challenges and the appreciation of reaching those small goals should be celebrated.

Gamification gives us instant rewards. This is an example of something that may cause a lot of frustration. Instant rewards are not natural, they are man-made. We just love it, but it's not what you should expect in the beginning of your journey. The obstacles you will meet are necessary for your success and more immediate rewards may be longed for, but the future rewards will be a lot greater than the ones you didn't have to work on to achieve.

Rewards you need time to achieve make you feel so much stronger. They give you the feeling of being someone closer to yourself and the feeling lasts longer; you are alive. These rewards are the fuel you need to keep on moving toward the next goal, the next level of success. That's fun and I highly recommend it.

Whatever you define as being fun is fun, but don't be surprised if you suddenly start to have fun when preparing your new lifestyle. ... and I almost forgot, it is also fun to play as if you already were having the success you are looking for. Pretend you are dressed as you want to be, pretend your house is of the standard you want; invite people to a masquerade where you decide what they should be wearing and the theme for the evening. That is fun, too. You should at least play with the idea, then find your own way of preparing for your success. A dream is a dream as long as you don't take action on it. When you take the necessary action, you enter your very own fairytale. Ask very old people about their regrets in life, and most of them will answer, "What I didn't do."

Do this now: *Find the spots during your week when you know you are having a good time with some people. It might be family, it might be friends. This time should be kept as it is. You don't want to change that, but you do want to measure it.*

(When you define that time, you will easily take the time off from everything else (there will always be exceptions, but make them as few as possible), make sure it gets good and make those good moments a part of your fuel for success.)

Time to take action!

SLEEP AND HOW
IT MAKES YOU BETTER

Sleep is underestimated. You need the sleep you need, no more, no less. The amount of sleep you need will never be found in a study (apart from some rough estimates), unless you do the study yourself. It's very easy to do this study and the results can prove to be very valuable. I'm not a medical expert, so if you're having huge problems sleeping, get the advice from someone who can give you answers.

I used to panic about sleeping, especially after talking to people who slept a lot more than I did. I never had the chance to graduate from the course of sleeping, it was always cancelled or maybe I was just too late. I never got to the lesson titled *"now it's time to go bed."* I kept wondering, *"when is a good time to go to bed"* and since no one told me, I just had to go to bed when I got tired.

Your body tells you that "you should close your eyes now". It is a message from the body to your brain that you need to give it some time to do some repairs, adjustments, calculations of what you should do next, find the solution you need to finish your project and a lot more. The system is amazing, but very often disrespected. When the body has finished its tasks, you get a signal. It opens your eyes for you. That is the signal of not needing to sleep for a while. You may not be fully awake, but the maintenance that needs sleep, is finished. You can continue.

When you sleep, your mind and body solve what you are not capable of solving. It takes a lot of energy to make a decision. Some decisions and adjustments are so demanding that the body needs access to a lot of energy to solve it properly. You get tired. This doesn't mean that you should sleep all the time; it means that when you have a problem you can't solve, you need your own help. If you're doing physical work, your muscles need rest and when you're doing mental work, your brain needs rest. Rest is doing something else, but we don't control it, consciously. Our subconscious knows a lot more than we know and controls our inner lives. I hope you enjoy your heart beating. If you're brain and body shut down while sleeping, there would never be another heartbeat.

Your subconscious knows what you need to do; it knows how to make you walk, talk, what to eat, how to balance and so much more than you think of. You are not capable of making those decisions consciously. It saps too much of your energy. When you sleep, or at least relax, your subconscious calculates what to do, based on all the experience you have in life. This is not a scientific description of what's happening, but what we need to understand to make sleep a helpful instrument instead of an obstacle.

I know this sounds weird for some people. You want to have control over when it is time to go to sleep, and in a way you do have control. Most of the time we schedule it, and by taking enough actions, the body, mind and soul want to sleep at the time you scheduled. You choose to listen to the signals your body gives you or you choose not to. If you don't, you are wearing out your body unnecessarily. It makes your mind and body less capable of doing what is best for you. Your mind and your body are your best friends, or perhaps a single friend – they are one. They do what you tell them, and they let you know when it's time for you to let them do the job. Trust your mind and your body; respect the signals and do whatever it is in your power to do to follow them.

"Yeah, right!
I am tired, but I have to finish this now; this problem must be solved!!!"

Trust your mind and your body. Make sure you clearly understand the problem; go to sleep. When you wake up, you will have a better solution; you'll be rested and you will finish it in less time than you would if you were up late, tired, designing a worse solution. This is an experience that many people have had who made the decision to cooperate with themselves.

TAKE CONTROL AND MAKE YOUR LIFE

We react very differently to sleep, but we still need it. There are periods when you are so pumped up that you forget to lie down and sleep; you are not tired. This means that your mind and body give you permission to continue. Accept that you don't need to sleep that much during these periods. If you never sleep, it is a problem, but if you sleep naturally, it's completely fine. Not forever, of course.

The more you care for your health, including sleep, the longer you live. The longer you live, the more of your own success you will see. It's in your interest to make your body rest and recover when it tells you so. You don't have to sleep, if your body does not need to. It's like putting children to bed because it's time, no matter how much fun they're having. They won't sleep anyway, so why not allow them to play a little more (within reason, of course).

You are no different. When you feel the need for a nap, your body tells you to make some adjustments; it needs some time for system maintenance, even if it is in the middle of the day. When you are learning a lot of new skills, your body wants to keep up. It does that by making adjustments here and there, and this is what happens when you sleep or at least relax.

You don't have to work late to succeed; you have to work smart.

PRACTICE USING YOUR TIME WISELY

There is something about our planning that is frequently forgotten. We do remember it every now and again. Some people are incredibly good at it, but most of us are not. You can usually see the difference in the way they manage their days. They get so much done, and you just stand there with your mouth open, wondering "How did she do that?" I might have written "he", but usually it is a "she". Women are better organizers than men. No, it's not my idea. Tradition, science and experience show it.

Now I distracted you, so let's get back to what it is that we forget. You probably guessed it, it is the time we should spend to have a great time with our nearest and dearest loved ones. This is partly right. We decide *when*, but very often we forget the *what*. It's like setting a date and a time, and nothing else. How often do you do that when you schedule something? I hope you didn't say always...

We need to practice everything that is new. There are always some habits to learn, some to improve and others to get rid of. To develop a habit we want, we need approximately 21 to 30 days. I wish I knew where I learned that, but I don't. What I do know, based on my own experience and the experience of a lot of other people, is that it's true. It is not just a guess. This is the time the brain needs to introduce the new program, wipe out and replace the old program.

We easily revert to old habits if we don't practice the new ones. First we have to do what it takes to make sure the reprogramming works; then we need to keep up the new habits on a daily basis to make sure they become solid habits. It wouldn't make sense to spend hundreds of hours to learn a skill and then just leave it without using it. Athletes or musicians would spend many hours improving their skills and then, often while improving, use the new skill while continuing to practice. Training makes you stronger and when you practice long enough, like in continuously, you will end up doing things automatically. Maybe you will need to make some adjustments here and there, but the more you practice, the better you get. This works with time as well.

If you are used to spending five minutes more than you should, just because you usually do it, you should change that. You can find a way to change what you do so you work five minutes smarter or you just stop. Getting into the habit of respecting your own time can make the difference between online success and online failure. If you could spend those five minutes here and there on building your online business, you could easily surprise yourself by the amount of work you get done in that time alone. Remember that resting is just doing something else. There is never nothing going on.

THE TECHNOLOGICAL OBSTACLES

"To climb steep hills requires
slow pace at first."
- William Shakespeare

YOUR KNOWLEDGE ABOUT THE TOOLS

Some knowledge is very basic, like turning on your computer, charging the batteries, opening programs and more. The tools you handle automatically are the easiest tools to use. Then come the tools you sometime use, either because you have used them frequently or you are familiar with them. The third group of tools are the new ones. You will always need to learn some new ones. The more you know about the tools, the better.

Learning something new has nothing to do with comfort, it has to do with doing. Humans, like you and me, are creatures of habit. We like to do what we like because we know how to do it and it passes the time. I've never met a person who loves to do what he or she doesn't like. Still we have to do these things sometimes; it is avoidable. It doesn't have to last for too long, though, and you don't have to dislike everything that is new for a long time.

Habits are strange. They protect us by being a result of our experience. We act like we do, because our habits permit it. This makes us feel so comfortable, and we have a great time, because we know what we are doing.

Sometimes we get into trouble, but we can solve it by acting like we usually do.

If this doesn't feel like you, there is a possibility that you are one of the people who act like you always have, but don't understand why you're not having a great time. You can also be one of the people who knows that what you are doing is wrong for you. Either way, you know that your habits protect you, because they always have. It's just that you stick to them, but you may not know why. In these cases, you are probably going to find a solution when you read on. If not, read it again and look for your answer between the lines, not in what is written as words.

Did you ever hear about someone not looking forward to the weekend? Have you ever had a problem with looking forward to the weekend? Usually people do look forward to the weekend, because we can spend time as we like. This also means we don't look forward to a Monday (if you have a regular Monday to Friday kind of job). Whenever you are not going to work, even if you like your work, you look forward to the time you have at your own disposal. Daily and weekly, not to mention the holidays.

How do habits and learning something new relate to my skills?

In every way. Your habits will make sure that you do not want to learn something new. As an example, when we are tasked with doing something new, all our alarms are turned on full blast: "We never did this before, so we are not going to do it." You can change this, and you should do so. This, after all, is a major reason why people don't succeed in online marketing. They stick with what they have always done and believe they will succeed. If they didn't succeed before, why should they succeed when sticking to what they always have done?

Your skills, every one of them, are exactly what they are because you did what you did. If you never did anything in online marketing before, you need to learn everything you need to do. If you're not interested in that, you can always pay for the service and have someone else do it for you, but in the end you would have to learn it so they don't take advantage of the situation. You need to learn something and you can learn to want it.

The funny thing is that you can use your habits to make things work consistently and develop a consistent action. First you need to know what you already know and what you can do. You can also outsource the right elements. This can help you to keep your happiness intact and save you time. Always welcome the lack of frustration.

Do this now:

1. _Make a list of all the skills you have on using a computer. Computers are very useful when doing online marketing, while tablets and phones are not. They come in very handy for other parts of your marketing. (There are exceptions to this rule, but in general this is the way it is). Here are a few examples of what to write, " I am a skilled writer", " I am good with numbers", "I am great at searching the web", "I'm good at implementing the use of new software," "I am ....." . Every little detail you can imagine for this task is great._

2. *Make a list of all the skills you have personally (repeated skills from previous chapters, as well). You can take it to any level you feel comfortable with. You may write, "I am a smiling person", "I am a money magnet", "I am good at eating with knife and fork", "I'm good at playing with the kids in the street", "I'm good at cleaning the house", "I'm good at watching the snow fall in winter". There are no limits for how long this list can be, it's your choice and you are good at a lot of things. I know; I'm human, too. If in trouble, ask someone who knows you and write down what they say you are good at. Do not edit what they say, accept it and appreciate it. You will need this list later.*

Secondly you need an idea of what you have to learn. After reading the four first chapters you might have some ideas already, it's time to manifest them.

Do this now: *On a new piece of paper, write down everything you believe you have to learn. If in doubt, write it down.*

The third step is to make new habits by using combinations from these lists. For now, you should just play with them and see what you come up with. Surprise yourself.

Time to take action!

RUN YOUR BUSINESS WHILE YOU DEVELOP YOUR SKILLS

One of the best ways of learning new skills and improving them is to use them for real, at once. The real time training keeps you alert about what you do on a completely different level, more so than you would be if you just made small attempts on your own. When you know that someone else will see it, you work smarter (because you know someone else will see it) and you will probably be surprised by the speed with which you learn the skill. Every time you use your skill, you will get better, work faster and smarter. If you keep it to yourself, your awareness might be less present, meaning that you spend a lot more time than you need to learn your skill. This might just as well result in no result at all. When you lose track of the intense joy of learning something new, and you never get any result from what you do, you are closer to the threshold for giving up. In the end, this means that you will go around saying "I tried, but it wasn't for me...". That's not what you want.

Getting a result, making it work and then starting to adjust it is a better way of working. First, you are more likely to get customers from something that exists than from something that just is an unfinished product or campaign.

Using your excitement for learning while you are creating something not only makes you learn faster, it also yields visible results faster, and this in turn will get you more customers sooner.

SOCIAL CONNECTIONS AND THE PRACTICAL CONSEQUENCES

The people surrounding you, have an impact on how you work. They can be the most important people in your life, and you may have a lot of fun together. You may have great colleagues and you may have some who are not so great. Either way, they influence you and you influence them. You get a clear picture of this when one is away. The atmosphere among the remaining colleagues changes. Everyone responds to the kind of group you're in, and when the group changes, you can feel the difference in the group.

Your contact with other people makes your mood swing a lot. If you are aware of the influence, you will start noticing the difference between when the time is good for keeping up with your friends and when it is time to leave. You need to believe strongly when you do your online marketing. It's not a problem when you have found your way of doing things, but it can be a problem when you are searching for your inner passion. The people around you can be supportive, which is great; the opposite is not. When you notice that someone doesn't believe in what you are doing, you should not listen to them, you should leave them out of it. Don't talk to them about what you do; you will not get support. When you get a stronger mindset, as we will see in the next chapter, this will get easier. At first, there are enough situations that leave you with questions. You don't need non-supportive people who can do more harm than good.

Your vulnerability is not very well concealed when everything is new, so by keeping a distance (I didn't say forever, that's something you need to consider later.) from the non-supportive people, you will most probably reach your goals faster. You need to take care of the people supporting you, because working alone can be very hard, still fun, but having someone to talk to about your progress and your achievements makes it a lot easier.

PROCRASTINATIONS

Doing something else without results?

For a long time I have observed myself procrastinating, and I find it interesting. There should be no need to say that "I didn't have time" to make notes or some such thing; after all, I was procrastinating. There had to be a solution to stop the procrastination, so I studied myself, and took the notes when I was done procrastinating.

Why I studied myself?

I had to, because I wanted to get rid of the procrastination. The most peculiar things happen when you study yourself, and this was no exception, I discovered something. Procrastinating isn't always procrastinating. So far, I have found two other reasons for this kind of behavior, and neither has anything to do with procrastination. They are easily misunderstood as procrastination, but they both have to do with attention.

When you are caught up in doing your own marketing, making your own campaigns, products or whatever, you easily forget the third and very important point I found. Every problem has a solution and it is always solvable. Let's first agree on the characteristics of procrastinations.

To get an idea of what procrastinations are, you could imagine yourself having a task set for delivery in three weeks. The first week goes by; you had so many other matters to take care of that "you were unable" to start on the task. What you did do, if you are a procrastinator, was to measure how much time was needed and concluded that there was more than enough time.

At the end of week two, you would be way off on another project or another task. At the arrival of the third week, you get a few hints about the original task, how you're doing, if you have the progress to get there in time. You normally do, unless you have found an even more exciting project or task to work on...

The expert procrastinator has the whole project or task in the mind, but never lets it get any further. When it's solved, it's done; you don't have to do anything more about it. You can move on and have new ideas, think it out, even dream them up and stop the project when you see the end result, without doing anything. Well, this doesn't exist either, it exists only in your mind. If you don't do anything about it, nothing happens.

To get the complete picture of what procrastination is, you need to be a procrastinator. This will give you first-hand knowledge of why you procrastinate and how it works. It is usually called making excuses for not doing what you are supposed to do. The results may vary a lot.

It doesn't matter whether you are passionate about it or not, it's just a way of doing something else than you should have done before, done according to someone else, usually not yourself. At least, the latter is used as an excuse, which makes it a double procrastination.

For some reason procrastinating often occurs when you have a deadline. A deadline is a word most commonly used in the media. There are some that argue that it originates from the Civil War prisons, this is not the time and place to argue about that, they might well be right. If they're wrong, however, it still doesn't matter, because what we need is the word in the sense it is used here. Let's use it as an example.

In prison, you were not supposed to cross the deadline, you would die. In newspaper jargon, it's the time limit for when to deliver something you want printed that day. If you deliver after the deadline, it may not be printed at all, unless it is very, very good.

Deadlines causes some kind of stress in a lot of people, meaning they do deliver before the deadline, simply to avoid the consequences that would occur if you didn't. Thanks to the effect this has on people, deadlines have been set everywhere. Which is very stressful. Everyone wants to do their best, not just something that is marginally adequate. With a deadline, most people get so worried that they won't deliver on time. The more you think about the deadline, the less focus you have on what you do. The less focus you have on what you do, the worse the material gets. In other words, deadlines make people deliver something they are not happy about. (Those who can live with deadlines are of course better at delivering something at least adequate). With practice, this ends up going well, for most people. You get used to it and you get a feeling of how much time you have left to make it great.

Deadlines are interesting in this context, because procrastinators have a very special relationship with them; they know they are there, but they don't see the problem.

This leads us into another misunderstanding of procrastinators. They are not necessarily sloppy or lazy. There is a bigger chance they are perfectionists. Procrastinators are more likely to skip doing something because they didn't see a good enough or perfect solution, more often than because they didn't do something.

You can never do nothing. You are always doing something. What you do may not be related to what you were supposed to do, as it appears. How things are supposed to be done and what you are supposed to do are less interesting parameters than doing what you are actually doing.

That is what happens. You do something that is more important for you to do, when you do it. On more than one occasion I have discovered that what I did instead led to a much better result than what would have resulted if I did what I was expected to do. Procrastination can just as easily be you seeing, subconsciously or even unconsciously, a solution that is far better than what you would present if you did merely what was expected. This is you taking responsibility for making the result as good as possible. It looks a lot like procrastination but should not be labeled as such. This yields results; procrastinations do not.

Procrastination is still doing something else because you don't want to do what you were supposed to do and the result is no result, at least not something you feel happy about.

The other way of taking actions looking a lot like procrastination is the immediate start of doing what needs to be done to make sure you get to the results you want. Sometimes you have to learn something new; other times you need time to get all the parts of the puzzle to match before you can start on the tasks you were supposed to do. Very close to the deadline, you get it, you put the pieces together and you deliver as ordered. If you don't, you might have procrastinated ...

THERE IS ALWAYS A SOLUTION

A deadline is not very scary for the professional procrastinator. They come and go. A procrastinator needs more focus on When to see the results, preferably without doing anything. If you have this kind of challenge, you can always make a result line instead of a deadline. It sounds a lot better and is something to look forward to. If you set the result line a week before the deadline, you may even find it fun to fulfill the tasks sooner than expected, you see the results and if you're not quite happy about it, you have time to adjust it.

Here is the solution so many people forget. In many cases, procrastinations occur because you don't know how to do something or where to start. There will always be someone else who knows. If you don't know anyone, you can always outsource the part of the workload that makes you insecure. You can always buy the service from someone else. They will be happy to help. It's a win-win solution. You get what you want, without doing it and your new partner or business associate gets paid for a service well done. This way, you can continue doing what you are good at and make your workflow steady, reach your target easier and smile.

CELEBRATE!

Celebrations are important. When you have completed something, you should celebrate. It doesn't have to be a big party; all you need is to raise your arms in the air and say a loud "YES! I did it!". This is almost the smallest one, you can also just whisper it to yourself while clenching your fists. Anything that is a victory should be celebrated, and if you do it often, you inspire yourself to move on.

One of the hardest things about working alone at home is the fact that you are alone. You have to make all the decisions; you have to learn all the skills; you have to make all the content and tend to lots of small details to make it work. When I phrase it this way, it sounds like a problem, but it isn't. You just need to be prepared for it. Everything is a little difficult in the beginning, but when you get used to it, you don't even think about it, you just do it.

Here is what you do:
Everything that looks big and difficult can be broken down into smaller parts. Collect the pieces and reassemble them. If you have to learn a program, you want an idea of what parts you have to learn. Take one thing at a time and use what you learn in the program and learn it as you assemble a campaign or a product you can use. Every time you see a connection, it's time for a

small celebration. If you do it, it gets easier to move along to the next. Celebrate and move on.

When you have done the complete campaign, learned everything you need in the program, managed to set it all up, tested it and ensured that it works, it's time for the bigger celebration. Deciding before you start can be a very good idea. Setting the goals, the time and a date sets up a reward for yourself. By celebrating, you reduce the harm many of these obstacles can do. You are in charge and you keep yourself going by always confirming to yourself that you can do this.

You should, because You Can Do This.

Next best steps!

If you haven't done all the tasks in this chapter, you should review them and do them. They will help you become more aware of what you really want and it will help you to get around some of these obstacles.

Now that you have done them all, you should start sorting out what you are good at and when you can do the work.

> *1 Schedule your time: The timetable showing when you can work, how much time you are able to work now (which you want to increase later), the time you have already scheduled with your friends and family, sports and more.*

> *2. Make a list of what you are good at and what you need to learn: You have your list covering computer skills, your personal skills, and the list*

of what you believe you have to learn (just the things you know you need for now; it will help you to get an idea of how much time you need).

3. You may have an idea now of something with which you want to start your online career. Use what you have and play around with your skills and your time. Make a serious attempt to get a picture (even a faint one is good) of your business. What is it people want when they visit your online store. How do you welcome them and how do you make sure you take care of them?

4. Do a search on the Internet. Search for the most natural question your customers would ask (in your opinion). Look at the top ten websites and decide what you would want to do differently. What will your online appearance look like, and how will it attract the people you want?

Time to Celebrate!

... and then you go to the next chapter to build a winning mindset!

Chapter 6

DEVELOP A WINNING MINDSET

"*I have come to believe that the whole world is an enigma, a harmless enigma that is made terrible by our own mad attempt to interpret it as though it had an underlying truth.*"

- Umberto Eco

I had to ask, "Where do I start?" The answer came to me quite quickly. Start where you are. "Why?", I asked. I was told how important it is to accept what you are and what you have. How crucial it is to know how you see yourself and what values you have. I felt that chill run down my spine, the one telling me that I don't want to know.

Simultaneously, I had an urge to know. I was split in two and in the middle was everything I had experienced, good and bad, funny and sad. I wrote a list of words, some sentences and a few drawings. After a while, I began to see the picture. It revealed how I saw myself, how I wanted others to see me, why I did what I did, some of my values and a lot of episodes I had forgotten, good and bad, funny and sad. Time to move on. Life is too short not to be lived. I found that Now was a good time to start. When life tells you to make some changes, then make some changes. Follow your heart.

You are not good when you are new at something, but you will be. During my years as a music teacher I have had the pleasure of seeing people become good. It has to do with practice and the proper training. When my pupils are new, I work hard to make them understand that they need to practice, preferably every day. That small step can be very hard, especially if you are uncertain of what you want. It can easily become a huge challenge to get into the habit of just doing it. The moment you manage to focus on getting there, you will notice that you get better. There is a small, but very important detail around this matter. You should constantly keep an eye at the goal, but at the same time, you should look back and see where you were a week or a month ago. In my teaching this has been very important, to make sure that my pupils see the difference between where they are and where they were. I just wish they all took the opportunity to improve themselves that way, but humans are humans. We are at different stages in life and we don't take the action until we have to or find ourselves ready for it.

It's just like anything else in life. We may know what we want, but since we don't know how to get there, we leave it at that point. It's a habit we have. When we want it bad enough, we act differently. We do what it takes to get it, based on what we have available. We do more, we start changing our habits to make sure we get the most out of it and when we have what we wanted, things gradually fall back to the way they used to be. The bigger the challenge, the more effort to conquer it and then we become acquainted with it and the excitement dissolves. The awareness of this fact should make you wonder why you are where you are in your life. It's a result of everything you have done and experienced in life. If life's great, be happy and grateful. If you don't have a great life, you can prepare to become the person you need to be to have a great life. What you want to have is attained by doing what it takes, but to stay there, you need to know who you want to be. Then you can avoid the setback and keep life great. It takes practice, but when you practice, you make it a habit. Imagine you having a habit of being great, and if you have, how about even greater?

Practicing is about repeating the same actions over and over, until they are under your skin. When we play the trombone (or any other instrument), we have a set of exercises we keep repeating until we are ready to go to the next step. By changing the exercises into more challenging ones, we constantly improve as long as we keep practicing. To get there, you need to be consistent. You can always be better by working forward and look back to see how much closer you are to your goals. This way you understand the amount of time needed to gain the knowledge you need to perform any piece of music, and that equals the making of an article or a campaign for your website.

It took a while before I saw the similarity between these two seemingly very different ways of working. They are not different. I found that teaching people how to play an instrument is the same as teaching yourself how to get going. I could use the same steps I used in my teaching to keep up the action in my marketing. You get the experience of knowing how good you can get. When you keep practicing, you constantly get better, even though it doesn't feel like it. Getting better is the result of doing the same actions over and over (like repeating the words as I just did, it's actually a great affirmation. Say to yourself; "I love doing the same actions over and over again, I rinse and I repeat." many times every day and you will notice a difference), just make sure you do what serves you and what works. In the end, or maybe way before, you are the expert and you master the skills without blinking. The hard part is usually not to understand this, but to do it. To make sure you get there, you need a strong mindset, especially when you work alone. You are the one to inspire yourself and you are the one to make sure you succeed.

Whether you do something or not, you are changing. The question we need to Ask ourselves is who makes the decision. If you let the days go by because that's what they do, you won't have a feeling of the direction you're heading towards. Your decisions will be based on others' decisions. Sometimes that is great, but you want to be the one who accepts it, not just the one that has to take the consequences.

The following is the importance of having a strong mindset. I discovered that I had a better feeling of what works and what doesn't after I started working consistently on my mindset. Daily I performed several small "rituals" during the day. I grew fast and I found myself strong enough to go for what I believed in. I didn't hesitate, I took immediate action and the results became noticeable immediately.

Being in control of my time makes it easier for me to get what I want. Another benefit is that I become more quickly aware of what is right for me to do. My teaching has become a lot more focused on what really matters, my life is constantly getting better and magical moments appear to happen more often.

The more consistently you work on your mindset, the faster you will notice the changes. You set your goals, big and small, both are important. You start being aware of what happens around you and you see what is good for you and what is not. This is important. You want to keep what is good and get rid of what doesn't serve you anymore.

Daily work on your mindset will make you understand the power more clearly a lot sooner than if you just take a session every now and then. One of the most important ways of training your brain is reading, listening and then take the necessary actions. You should read daily about what works for your mindset. Successful people, no matter what they do, no matter what their success is, have a habit of reading about success and constantly clearing their mindset. Lending an ear to others' successful experience is a way of constantly searching for new perspectives, it opens your mind to see things differently and suddenly you have the answer to all your challenging questions.

When you are taking the right actions, you are building your habits into the action takers' paradigm. This is a way of turning dreams into reality, just by maintaining and improving your everyday life. You might look at it as having service done on a car. When you follow the services recommended, you will always have a car that works. Everything is fixed before it has a chance to get broken. When you train your mindset daily, you are having "service" on your brain. You will love the results.

THE HUNT

There are several ways of developing a winning mindset. I know many marketers who believe that watching a motivational video serves the purpose. It helps, but if you don't dig as deep as you can, you don't really get the mindset. You're easily fooled. Having a winning mindset means, among other things, that you are capable of making the right decision at the right moment. If you don't have a winning mindset, you can still be successful, but you are also a lot more vulnerable. You may feel fine for a while, but when the going gets tough, you may find yourself in lack of the power you need to continue.

Your winning mindset is somewhere within you. What you need is to become aware of it and practice using it. You want to find your real purpose and you want to be good at picking up the signals that get you there. When you get good at it, when you sense what is the right thing to do, you will know it's right.
Knowing is a lot better than just guessing or choosing what someone told you you're good at. We are all good at many things, but that does not mean we want to do them.

Your awareness helps you make the right decisions when you need them.

Your enigmatic travel on earth becomes less and more enigmatic at the same time when you are searching for your winning mindset. It becomes less enigmatic because you get used to it and more enigmatic because you discover new connections. You see a bigger picture and you understand more the importance of every little detail. The deeper you go, the more good qualities you find in yourself and you discover why you are good at what you are really good at. The more you know, the more fascinating the hunt for the "better you" becomes.

There are turns and curves, ups and downs, backwards and forwards, but these are all just the directions you need to take to get to the best you that you can be. Instead of being surprised, enjoy the ride and always look for what you learn, what serves you and if there is anything else you can learn on the way. There is never a dull moment, it gets so exciting to see where you end up. Life become the most wonderful movie you've ever seen. Whether it's up or down, start looking and you will find something better in the other end. When the good days turn up again you've had such a great travel that your smile is even bigger and you start looking for the next challenge, the next ride.

... and for how long do I have to keep up this exhausting excitement?

Too many people just go for the "this is not for me"-attitude. Well, that's just the old you, all your habits and feelings that you have allowed to control you. Some are good, some have been good and some are bad. You want to keep the ones that still serve you, but you want to get rid of those that don't. When you're honest with yourself, you will know which ones to keep and which ones to let go. It's not hard, if you're honest, but if you try to fool yourself, it can be really tough. The more you know, the better you get and the better your life will be. An abundant life is best achieved when you follow your passion, your heart and use your winning mindset to control your actions and adjust them according to changes around you. This is for you, and this is what you really want. Why not go with the flow instead of fighting it?

When you understand why you want to improve who you are, you also have an understanding of what you want to do with your life, at least what you want to do at the stage where you are right now. There is no need to panic if you find that you have to do something you never did before. Your search will always show you a path you've never walked before. It's like magic, you start doing things you never thought of doing, and you love it. Sometimes you will feel down, but that is just a feeling, you may want to find the reason, but you don't have to follow it. You are doing it already.

It's like being in a gathering, you are wearing your finest clothes, you feel great and it's important for you to be there. You talk about your success and how exciting it is to learn this new technique of launching your product. Everyone wants to hear what you are talking about, and there is a good feeling in the room. Some unfortunate person stumbles next to you and you are the one getting splashed with juice ... (*know the feeling?*). You were taken by surprise, to put it mildly, but instead of throwing what's in your glass in this person's face, now embarrassed, feeling sorry, wanting to make everything right, you say it's all right, you are grateful for the help you got to clear off the worst. Let all your feelings go and start getting back into the conversation. You could have chosen something else, some do, but you always have a choice.

Everything we do teaches us something we need. We need it to make our lives better, and the more we search, the more we find. Just remember to take action on what you discover and you'll get more targeted. Being aware of what life can bring is very powerful and makes you a lot stronger on days when everything seems to go wrong. Things don't go wrong; they just take a turn that you need to take to get to your destination. Your winning mindset will then show you how to turn things in your favor. Your brain is very powerful and when you use it for Your own good, instead of someone else's, you will see yourself sailing through life (still with ups and downs, but not so deep downs; even they can be very exciting, never frightening). This is a lifelong process, but you can improve rapidly and instantly, if you permit yourself, not even the sky has to be a limit. We can always be better at something, and we do improve. Every one of us. No exceptions.

BE AWARE OF
WHAT YOU DON'T WANT

We must let go of the life we have planned,
so as to accept the one that is waiting for us.
- Joseph Campbell

The world is full of options. There are so many options
that we easily get confused. Most people give up trying
and merely follow what everyone else does. A few others
follow their passion, without knowing it. It's just a
natural way of pursuing their lives. The rest, actually
most people, make the best choice based on what they
know or what other people seem to have done
successfully. The surprising moment is always when you
discover that you don't succeed the same way. Why does
that happen, you may wonder?

Here's what I discovered:
Picture yourself driving a car in a roundabout. You are
somewhere in the five-lane roundabout, trying to figure
out how to get out of there. Slowly you get one more lane
closer, then one more but you're still driving around, you
get so used to being in the roundabout, you almost forget
you are on your way out. You get to the outer lane, but
keep repeating the turns, following the car in front, not
thinking about the fact that the driver probably is just as
confused as you. You see your exit, but being so focused
on the traffic, you forget to turn the wheels the other way.
You have to go for another round, you start focusing on
getting out of there, you "wake up", get to your exit, and
makes the most perfect exit you have experienced, you
are so grateful and happy for the fact that you made it...

There are many times during my lifetime when I have found myself in a roundabout. Simply repeating one day on the model of yesterday, without even looking for changes. After a while, I discovered that weeks had passed by, more or less completely without my presence. You have probably been there yourself. It's as if all your senses have been sleeping; you just find yourself in a vacuum and wonder what happened. In my case, this was usually because I was off track in my own life. I was following instructions from others, leaving myself out. I stopped noticing what really happened around me and as a result, I stopped appreciating the things I really cared about. Even worse was when it didn't matter anymore. Those periods, walking in this roundabout just made me so dizzy that everything had lost its meaning and value in my life... The last time I "woke up" from such a roundabout, I was luckily only on my way into it. I built a terrace, found a way out, established a direction and started a journey I wouldn't trade for anything.

I believe both you and I know people who have been in worse situations and experienced this, people who lost their job, experienced a family break-up, long-term illness and so much more. Each of us has experienced this in one way or another, some more existentially than others, some more dramatically than others. It does give color to life, or a shade of color or a scar... but how do we solve it, how can we escape it?

Passion is the answer, combined with a strong mindset and determination to get there. If you experience an awakening, wondering what to do, or wondering about whether you need to do something, you're either on the wrong end of your passion or you're far removed from your passion. Your mindset gives you directions on how to live Your life, not someone else's, but distractions and lack of making decisions keep us away.

Seeing the importance of life makes us start this journey into freedom. We set one foot in front of the other and take the first bold step toward our new self. We gradually become aware of the fact that we didn't do more. We stopped after the first step, so happy for the quest for a better and improved self that we forgot to continue; nothing more happened. We just took a different lane in the traffic circle, made the world look a bit different, just one or two lanes closer to the exit, but still in the traffic circle.

When you want to develop a winning mindset, there is one approach that gets you closer than other ways. There is a set of actions to start implementing. If you try to change everything at once, you will only get confused and probably exhausted, almost like reading a map without understanding the drawings or the symbols. Quite similar to reading a book in a language you didn't know existed. The actions are supported by your handwriting (preferably), just to make yourself more focused on what you do.

Writing down what's on your mind, makes it easier for your mind to sort what you both remember not to forget AND try to move into the right type of experiences. You should start by writing down everything you do not want in your life. When you write it down you free some of the energy you're using to remind yourself that you don't want it in your life. This energy can then be used for the hunting of what you want. We get easily distracted during our everyday life. When we get rid of the distractions, it gets easier to see what direction we should have followed.

Here is what happens:
Writing down the absolute obvious habits and fears in your life that no longer serve you triggers other habits and fears. The more you find, the more you understand why things have been different from what you wanted. It's like drawing a map of what is holding you back. When you are done, it's time to let them go; there is no need for them, so accept that they have existed and tell them goodbye. You remove what is stopping you and make it easier to find even more habits and fears you didn't know were there. They do not help you, whatever excuse you might find. They probably served you once, but no more. You will also find some that never served you, but got into your life because they served others. Make it very clear to yourself what you don't want in your life. Be very honest to get the best results.

What is the connection between "what I don't want" and a winning mindset?

When we do what we are good at, we do what we like or what we have become good at. This might even be the result of a fear of losing a job or any other kind of threatening factor. Training and practicing to become very good at something is not necessarily what we want to do. Did you ever say to yourself; "*it's just a job...*"? You may have trained your mind to do what you have to do to make the job as effortless as possible, but if you ask yourself that question, you are not on track with yourself. Life is full of threats. They usually start with, "If you don't do that, I will make sure you never...", or the much friendlier, "It's in all our interest that you do what you're told". It may seem harmless, but it is threatening. We automatically start considering the consequences and if they are too much to handle, there needs to be a change. What has to be changed, may not be what you agree on, but you can always be the responsible making the changes you need to act on. If you are doing what you do (and you may be good at it) for someone else's good; you are helping others realize their dreams. It's a very nice thing to do. You get your salary and you make sure someone's dream comes true, but what about your dreams?

You don't get the freedom to make them come true. Your dreams are not meant to be just dreams. They are signals for what you can realize in your life. You may need help to get there, and with a winning mindset, you will. What you don't want are the habits and excuses that stop you from achieving your goals. This doesn't mean you should stay away from helping others to reach their goals, it just means that your goals are equally important, no matter how big or small.

Your winning mindset will guide you in the direction of your newfound freedom. As you hunt for your passion, your mindset will make sure that you do what you need to do to get there. It's the subconscious taking responsibility for preparing you, just at the right time. When you take away all the distracting elements, like what you don't want to be and what you don't want in your life, you get a stronger vision of all the things you can do to make your life closer to the freedom you seek. When you get there, you will know it. If you already know it, take action on it now.

Are you telling me I'm inadequate?

You are good enough to do what you do now, but if you want some changes in your life, you need to change something. You can't pretend you are changing something and hope for a different result. If you are earning millions, you might be happy with that, but if you want to earn billions, you need to change something that makes you capable of earning billions. If you are earning a few thousand, then that is what you are good at. What you need to change varies from person to person, whether it includes earning several thousand more or millions more. Some are ready but don't know it. They need to be awakened: that is also a change. Others are definitely not ready. They have to change something else. They need to get rid of what is stopping them from earning more than they earn.

We all have different backgrounds, and we cannot get rid of that, but we can change the outcome of our background. We are bombarded on a daily basis with complaints, lack of confidence (not necessarily our own), fear of something or images that make us doubtful about what we can accomplish. They cast a pall or a doubt over our lives and this affects our behavior, our language, our thoughts and our beliefs. If we are unaware of these influences, if we don't know why we behave as we do – why we speak as we do, why our thoughts are what they are and what we believe in, we will become a part of all the things we don't want to be a part of. We start spreading what doesn't serve us or anyone else.

Our awareness determines our strength, mental strength as well as physical strength. You are adequate, but you can be better. I am no exception, You are no exception. None of us are. We can help each other by accepting other people for what they are and help them look for the possibilities instead of the limitations. The best way of helping is by being a good example without judgement. I have my life to maintain, you have yours. The next person is in the same situation based on his or her life.

BE AWARE OF WHAT YOU WANT

When you look at a forest, you may not see anything else but trees. When you walk in the streets, you may not see anything else but people passing by. Just like people, every tree has a role, a purpose. People, like trees, adjust their growth to get to their target. The trees may grow quite close to each other. When one stretches toward the sky, the others follow. It's as if they cooperate on getting taller, helping and protecting each other. The leaves and branches grow in a way that makes them get as much light as possible and they share the space between them. When one tree stretches a branch in one direction, the neighboring tree will stretch its branches in another direction. We take actions that make us stand out and make our days as meaningful as possible; if WE do not, we stagnate and rot inside, just like a tree would stop growing and get strangled if it doesn't keep making space for its branches together with the others.

During winter, the trees protect each other against the strong winds, keeping each other safe. By cooperating, they survive the hard winters, ready to drink water from the earth and grow bigger in spring. Their roots intertwine underground, helping each other to help each other. It is fascinating how they cooperate and I hope you have noticed that they are wonderful to look at. We have a lot to learn from trees.

The trees are not as different from people as we may think. We meet many people and we interact. We take our space, and we should. We make space for others; we care for each other, help each other as we should. We make a difference just by being. The more we do for others, the more meaning we bring to our own lives. The stronger your mindset is, the more you want to help others and you know the reason why.

Your role in your society may be something you feel is right. If you don't, it's time to make sure you find it, or maybe it's time to move on? Your mindset is capable of helping you. It's not about what you think, it's more effective if you don't try to do all the thinking. You can create the awareness, by using your memories. You remember what you did when you really had a good time. These memories can give you leads as to what you really want in your life, or teach you what you need to take the next step on your path.

Whatever you have decided to do with your life, you should not stop until you are there. Some of the time we all have our moments of "clarity". Everything we want to change is clear to us, like a vision, a solution, a desire to be someone that matters. We love our business, whether it's private or professional, and we want it to be something that matters. We love it when our lives matter. It is important for us to make our lives worth living. One of the obstacles in life is the simple fact that we merely keep on doing what we usually do. We like it so well that we may change a few things, but let ourselves be dragged into the same circle of life and we accept it. Life as it usually is, only with a twist.

Life doesn't have to be like that, there are ways of getting out of the rut, but you may not like it. You have to continue changing and never give up until you are where you want to be. By the time you get there, you will have new goals and a full tank of excitement. My life has been a lot of things – some good, some not so good, but there is a reason why I looked for and discovered a way out. I was tired of realizing that I was kicking my own butt. So what did I need to do?

I had to make permanent changes to make my life worthwhile. I wanted my life to be interesting for myself and at the same time, I wanted to reach out to others, lend a helping hand to others in the same position. My point was that I needed to learn something that was valuable for me and at the same time gave me an opportunity to help others in the same situation to help themselves. So when I found the right combination for doing this, I just kept on doing what I was told to do, and I got better, and I am still getting better every day. You will be surprised when you find out who keeps telling you what to do.

By continuing my changes, and continuing to change until I reach my goals (and by then having new ones), I manage to make my life meaningful, for myself and all the people around me, with the help of many people in the same situation. I just love being away from that traffic circle. You want this, too. You can decide to experience the same thing; it's your choice. Now is always a good time to start.

"You are here to enable the divine purpose
of the universe to unfold.
That is how important you are"

- Eckhart Tolle

BEWARE OF WHAT IS STOPPING YOU - THE LIMITING BELIEFS

Everything that makes you stop doing what you feel like doing is based on what is called limiting beliefs. They can be anything; they don't have a shape or form, but they do have an intention of stopping what you are trying to change. Why you believe or feel that your new changes are wrong would be a limiting belief. They can be words you heard in your childhood, at school, at work, among friends, on television, in a movie, in a theatre, in a song on radio or anywhere else. They are connected to something you have experienced or been told. They make everything around you look and feel very dangerous and scary, so your life gets pretty serious and difficult to live. You stay away from acting in certain ways because you don't believe it's good for you. They can be big, they can be small, but they stop you from doing something you haven't done before. Who wants to live a serious and difficult life?

Some people have chosen this way of life, a difficult or serious life. Maybe they grew up with it, getting the impression that this is the way life has to be. "This is how we have always done it", is a sentence heard more often than it does any good. Online marketing hasn't been around for so long a time that it qualifies as something that has been done for generations, so if you only keep doing what you always have done, you miss the biggest new opportunity there is, right now.

No one was born to have a difficult life, but when we experience difficulties, they mark us for a reason. We are supposed to learn from difficulties, not live them. Difficulties should be avoided, they don't serve us. Limiting beliefs are usually connected with fear of some kind. One of the most common among online marketers, is the fear of succeeding.

LIMITING BELIEFS

"I could never do that", "I'm too old", "this is too dangerous", "I can't afford it", "money makes people strange", "I don't need so much", "this is too difficult", "I'm not so good at talking to people", "I can't sell anything", "what would people say", are all common statements that people make. This is the perfect way of letting all the opportunities pass you by. These are just a few among thousands, and some are less obvious than others, but they are all what we call limiting beliefs.

You have probably had a great idea, let yourself think about it, smiled to yourself, and then let all the thoughts take over the show. First, you were convinced how fun it would be, but it ended with you thinking how impossible it would be. Limiting beliefs are very powerful. They can stop any dream from being realized. It's not your fault entirely, but since you had the idea, you were the one who should have taken the action. You even liked the idea.

The limiting beliefs come from all the influences we experience throughout our lives. Even when we are having fun. "You can't do that", marks us. If you believe you can do it or always wanted to, then you can do it. All it takes is the action to learn it. You can even be very good at it. People don't help us out here. They are used to seeing us doing what we usually do, so when we don't, they tell us we can't do that. What stops you are all these words. If you never had a chance to live out your passion, no one has ever seen you do it, they don't believe you can, you begin believing they are right. They are, of course, wrong. The fact that you can't, YET, stops you from even trying. The closer this negativism touches your passion, the more feelings you have on the subject. The more feelings, the harder it seems to even try. Still, You and only you, can change it. You Can Decide not to listen to all these people. You can start without them knowing and when you get good at it, you can surprise them. Whenever you react because of a feeling, you have discovered a limiting belief.

It may sound as if the limiting belief comes from other people. It doesn't, it comes from you. You tell yourself that you can't, and when you do, you are right. You can't. The moment you turn around and tell yourself you can, you are right. You Can. This is an inner game of self, and you control it, whether you like it or not. Usually we tell ourselves that we can't, for some reason. It's almost like we prefer not to succeed. At least it is easier to say that we won't make it happen than to tell ourselves we will make it happen. The difference, of course, is the action we need to take. If you say you won't succeed, it would be because you never intended to try. If you do what it takes, step by step, there is no need to doubt it. You will succeed. With your plan, you even have an idea of when it can happen. Limiting beliefs will turn up, but you can easily get rid of them.

When you are new to online marketing, you will experience a lot of new actions you have to take and new skills you have to learn. This, along with the insecurity of it being right or wrong, may cause you to feel you're not doing very well. This could be the result of a limiting belief. Your way of handling limiting beliefs can make a very big difference in your results. If you are very insecure about what you do, this will be revealed in your marketing. This doesn't mean that you are not able to succeed, it just means that you need to practice more and get confident in what you do. The more consistent, the better. If you are scared of learning something or doing something, it would be because of a limiting belief. You would recognize the feeling of being scared to take action. No feelings? No limiting belief.

Limiting beliefs are connected to our feelings. The way we feel when we take actions, the way we feel when we learn a new skill may bring forth some limiting beliefs. If it feels bad because you found it challenging, it may just be that you would like to know how to do this, and move on. A limiting belief would make you stop and think "can I do this?", try again, stop and think "I'm not sure I can do this" and this will continue until you say "I can never do this". Never allow yourself to get there; you can stop it the moment the first question pops up in your mind. This should be a wake-up call. The time to find a way to get rid of limiting beliefs is always RIGHT NOW. If you just had a bad feeling because you wanted to move on, then clench your teeth and keep on working on the challenge; you easily overcome the challenge by repeating the actions you had to take. That's actually a lot of fun, and it is not a limiting belief, it is your urge to be better. When you do many things you haven't done before, you are insecure; you are testing things. Some choices work out right while others take some time to become right. It's like life itself. If you managed to walk the first time you tried, you were either lucky or very prepared. Most of us had to fall

multiple times, to learn how to balance. When we did, we could walk, first one step, then maybe three...
You should look upon it as a small success when you discover you are good at something. If you feel it takes too much time to learn, buy the service, at least until you get good at it; then you can celebrate twice. How about that? First you celebrate when you publish your material and secondly when you get good at it. You can't celebrate too often, every day you should have a small celebration ceremony (it doesn't have to be a big party, a big smile and acknowledgement of your new skills is a great way of celebrating. A real Boost!).

There are other limiting beliefs, probably some of the reasons why you haven't started, YET. Many are looked upon as excuses, but they have a deeper meaning. They can be hard to discover, they are very nice and they don't seem to make a difference. In the end, they can be the ones that make you give up. You can change that and you start by being aware of why something inside gives you a feeling of something being difficult or maybe impossible. They are not. Split them into the smallest pieces and solve them, one by one. You can be the master of anything you want, but remember to be somewhat realistic about the time frame for the goal.

Some limiting beliefs have been there since childhood. The attitudes of grownups have dramatic impact on children. We are all influenced by the language, opinions, and attitudes of grownups during our childhood. Many of their limiting beliefs are more or less inherited. They meant well, but frequently you suffered. Sometimes things went very wrong. These limiting beliefs that were passed down from grownups can be anything – words or actions, words about you, about others, ways of doing things, ways of believing things and endlessly more.

Whatever stops you from doing what you want to do is connected to a feeling that implies a limiting belief. This is a reason to be careful about talking about others, for instance, especially when they can't be there to explain why they did what they did. Maybe they are trying to get on with their lives?

HOW TO BE RID OF
THE LIMITING BELIEFS

There are many ways to be rid of limiting beliefs. All the methods work, but maybe not for everyone. I've tested many different ways of getting rid of these obstacles, and most of them have met with success. You have a feeling of relief when they start losing their grip, and you should not be surprised if you start laughing more. The relief makes you happier and when you look back and see how things used to be, you might do more than just smile about it. Laughing is a natural response for happiness and we cannot laugh too much. Other people might get embarrassed, but try to make them understand and let them laugh too; it wouldn't hurt anyone. Actually, it would help everyone.

To be rid of a limiting belief, you need to accept its presence. It is important that you take it seriously. You should thank it for its stay, and wish it a happy journey now that it's leaving you. Make sure you leave it too. Usually there is a habit attached to it, and you don't want the habit to remain present either. Make sure that you happily wave goodbye to both the limiting belief and the habit attached to it. Yes, they need to go, and that is so important that I repeated myself.

VISUALIZE YOUR GOALS

*"Your future is only as bright
as your mind is open."*
— Rich Wilkins

When you know what is coming, you are prepared for it
and make it a good experience. Any experience can be
turned into something that keeps you going, because you
are prepared for it to happen. The clearer you can
imagine this by visualizing it — even better, if you can see
yourself being there, doing what you want and living how
you want to live — the more inspiration you get to make it
happen.

You don't plan for days to go wrong. Some days do
anyway and you can't do anything about it. Except for
one thing. With a good plan for your business, so detailed
that you can see yourself in the process of doing what you
want to do to make your life what you want, the bad days
don't matter; you still know you will succeed.

Nature, life and business all have their bright and dark
sides, but as long as you prepare for a bright and
promising future, you will see less of the dark sides and
more and more of the bright ones. Keep yourself updated
on your better self, stick with your plans through the days
of darkness and you will succeed in reaching your goals.

Small Changes can improve your life in ways you never
dreamed of...

Stop doing things "the right way", the way others told you was the right way. Change your perspective into a far more benefiting way of seeing things: Make life come to you and Give you the directions to make The Right Decisions.

Did you ever have that need to do something differently from what you usually do? Sometimes, when we have our guard down, relax and have the feeling of being in a kind of safe, protected state of mind, we get in touch with our true self. We don't shut ourselves down or hide ourselves in those situations. We are what's called open-minded and the most peculiar things can happen. If we are aware of those signals, we can learn a lot about ourselves; one lesson, among many more, is that by following the impulses these signals send, we can move our life in the direction it is meant to follow.

I know that some people find this way of thinking laughable. By making so many plans to accomplish everything on the to-do list, having more than ample events on the calendar and making sure you are never alone, you will never have the time to listen to yourself. The statement above does not make sense in those situations. It can't make sense with these terms because there is no room for your own life to guide you.

Many people choose that solution, so they don't have to make their own decisions on how to master living a good life, providing what's good for themselves and the people they want to share life with. By letting others control what you should do, you will get caught in their web. You might think that you are in the position to make your own choices, but you are so deep into other people's way of ruling your life that it's almost impossible for you to notice it.

If you start listening to yourself, give yourself the time needed to hear your own inner voice, you will be surprised by the direction and guidance you will get. Sometimes a small change can give your life a quantum leap (yes, I know they are very small, but the effect of those small leaps can change your life). Just a small adjustment can be the door opener to worlds you could only dream of entering.

You can experience this new life. You can get the guidance you need to get you through all the small signals. They will help you set your course to your destination, your goals. They will provide you with everything you want instead of you chasing them and never get any closer.

The better you get at visualizing your goals, feeling them, sensing them, touching them and hearing them, the more securely you will establish them. You are the creator of the moments and you can make them happen. When you add a flexible business like online marketing to your goals, you have begun your journey to a new way of living life, where you make all the decisions.

SURRENDER

When we have a clear picture of what we want, and we have a strong mindset to keep us focused and take the actions needed, it's important to make sure we use the strongest tool we have to keep us on the right track. Our subconscious mind can do incredible work for us, and if we let it, we will have greater ideas coming to us when we need them than if we try to think our way to success. Our conscious mind is occupied with dealing with all the bombardments from the outside, a huge mass of information to be sorted, all the time. In addition, it is occupied by being on the alert for possible dangers, so leaving the heavy lifting to our conscious mind gives us a result that can be great, but not guaranteed. Our subconscious mind gives us what we need when we need it.

The solutions are usually a lot better than you were able to consciously think. This is the reason why you should trust your subconscious to deal with your goals and give you your instructions. When you do, amazing things happen, and you don't need to worry about a thing. It all starts by leaving your visualized goals to your subconscious; "forget them", as in not worrying about how to get there. Make your plans as good as possible, but be open for signals for improvement all the time. Everything happens for a reason and you should let it happen and follow the signals.

Next best steps!

1. *Write down everything you don't want to be. If in doubt, write it down. You can change the list later. Your first challenge is to make yourself aware of all the possibilities and get rid of all the "noise" disturbing your winning mindset.*
2. *Write down everything you do want to be. It doesn't have to be an occupation. Everything you feel can define you, the way you want it to be, should be on that list. This can also be changed later. This exercise is a wake-up of*

your awareness, not the goal. You are on your
way; keep going.

3. *Search the Internet for limiting beliefs. There*
   are several methods; you should try them all.
   You may find some better than others; they all
   work, but they work differently for different
   people. Using different methods can also be
   healthy for variation. Make it a habit to let go of
   the limiting beliefs as soon as possible.

Chapter 7

HOW TO PRODUCE CONSISTENT RESULTS

CONSISTENCY

When you are doing something consistently, you get awesomely good at doing it. At first, we are awesomely clumsy, because we haven't learned it yet. Old habits have a grip on us. They don't necessarily make things easy for you, but when you have the opportunity to improve, you start wanting to change them. Habits are good and habits are bad. We want to keep the ones that serve us well, but we want to change the ones that no longer serve us. It may take some time, but it is absolutely possible to turn unproductive habits into ones that serve us. You can only get there by working consistently. The more often, the better, and daily practice is preferable.

We are raised in the same way, you and I. I know, there are differences, but in general, we are raised the same way. When we were old enough to go to school, we did; they told us what to do, and we did it. In school, we had to do both what they told us to do and the way they told us to do it, and we did. Not always, but then we got help, so we could do it the way it was meant to be. This could be a very long story, but the essence is that there are some terms and habits society wants us to learn. It is done consistently, because it is scientifically proven to be a great way of learning habits. All of these habits are needed to make your life a secure place to be, according to the system. Yes, to be. You exist in your life, so you have to be your life. Make your life yours and be the life you are, consistently.

The security you get from society is just as much for you to function together with all the people around you. You are taught ways of being flexible, but only flexible as in what you can do within the system to fulfill your position as a good worker. Among other things, you become educated to deal with other people. We are not alone, and we don't want to be alone all the time (with possible exceptions). We need other people around us; it is one of the functions we have, it is a part of us. This doesn't mean one has to be with people all the time. At that point, we are very different. School is meant to give us the training we need to interact with other people. Later, we get more advanced training at work, and we practice it at home, with friends, private or public celebrations and elsewhere.

These habits are sometimes beneficial to us but are sometimes what keeps us away from the life we are supposed to live. When we look into what these habits are, we can turn them in our favor. Since most people have been a part of the training you get at school, they react according to it, and when you know what they do, you also know something about how they act on different matters. It's a great move to accept this, that is, if you want to achieve consistent results in your business. If you don't like it, work on accepting it. You can't change it, at least not alone.

Everyone is your potential customer. They are all good people and everyone has their issues to solve, like you and I. We need to accept what is, to make our business work with people, our potential customers. Our habits should automatically welcome everyone and everyone should feel welcome, because we can solve one of their problems.

When we look at our own habits, we find some we like and some we don't. By studying each one of them, you will find which are serving you now, and which no longer serve you. This is about being honest with yourself.

Before we get to the consistent results, we need to know a little about the good and the bad habits. *"I know what a good habit is,"* you may think (or say), well, so did I, but habits are tricky. They don't want you to know they are there; they just want you to keep on doing what you usually do, whether it's good or bad. They don't care, as long as you do it the way they want you to. This makes some of your habits difficult to discover; they hide behind each other, so we have to dig a bit deeper. *"I don't want to go deep!"* The truth is, you do. Take one step at a time and you're fine, you can always take one step at a time, and you should. You'll be surprised by what you didn't know you do and why you do it.

Rome (Italy) wasn't built in a day; actually, they are still building. Time demands changes. Humans are constantly changing, even without us knowing what changes. Signals are absorbed in the brain and we change. We can always be better, but not without a change. Better makes us stronger and stronger makes us more capable of deciding what's right and what's wrong.

We need those skills to make consistent results.

BAD HABITS
- THE HABITS NOT SERVING YOU

Any habit can be good and bad, but if you think about it, you will find they are not. They just are. We are the ones determining whether it's good or bad, but a habit is just a habit. It all depends on how it serves you and the results of doing it. If you have a habit of giving away everything you own, it is a habit people like. They call it a good habit, and it serves a lot of people. If you have to starve to keep this habit, it doesn't serve you, so it will be a bad habit for you. This is the way you need to understand the challenges pertaining to habits; the good can be bad and some bad can be good. Habits are not necessarily easily spotted but the more we are aware of our moves and actions, by being present, the better we get at understanding what serves us and what doesn't serve us.

The first habits we keep away from are the ones that make a government pass a law against them. Those laws are meant to keep us away from something that doesn't serve us as a community. The laws may not always make sense to the public in general. Laws are made for the bigger picture, to help society stay on a desired course. You don't have to agree with the law, but you have to accept it. If you can't accept it, you will spend a lot of mindpower on a subject you can't do anything about. If you can do something about it, on the other hand, do what you can, but leave it when you can't do anymore.

Bad habits very often lead to other bad habits, and that is not what you want. When you discover your bad habits, big or small, you should take action and change them. Habits are changeable. We can change them into what serves us, instead of continuing to do what doesn't serve us. Like a law: We are not supposed to steal, so there is a law saying you will be sent to prison if you steal. Don't steal, and you'll be fine. Bad habits are not good for you. You are not supposed to do it. Change your actions, and you'll be fine.

There is (probably) no law against eating too much, drinking too much, never exercising, not sleeping enough, watching too much TV or disliking someone else. These are all habits that wear us out, meaning they don't serve us. We have habits we should stay away from, others should be reduced or changed to create a healthy balance. We sometimes even know it, but don't take action on it. Doing too much of anything wears us out. Eating too many carrots makes your skin turn another color than what is natural for you and is not healthy, even though carrots are healthy. Learning something new without taking breaks is not a smart move either, but learning something new is still a great move. Leaving out taking breaks, isn't. There are a lot of things we do for pleasure or maybe we inherit the habits that don't serve us. We may even know this to be true, but we still maintain the habits because that is what we usually do. When you constantly avoid taking care of yourself in your daily life, both mentally and physically, you have some habits that keep you away from your better self. When you actively and sometimes automatically search for negative solutions, you have some habits you want to change; they don't serve you, and they won't help you.

When we look inside ourselves, what we do, how we react, our awareness tells us what is good for us and what isn't. It might be a hard task to rid yourself of the habits you don't want, but we know we need to do so, and our success depends on it. The better the feeling, the more we are capable of focusing on what serves us. All the actions not making us feel good do something to ourselves and other people that should have been avoided. Accepting them as habits doesn't serve you anymore; you neutralize their influence, but you need to change your habits and widen your horizon to stop them from producing a new circle of negativity.

A bad habit is a habit that doesn't serve you anymore, and probably never did. Some habits just appeared suddenly, without our knowing why. We just started doing something, almost out of the blue. These kind of habits are usually triggered by the influence of people surrounding us. If all your friends eat a chocolate bar at 4pm, you probably do too. There are many small habits constantly and consistently eating away at your time and your wallet; you will be surprised when you discover them.

When you have discovered them and think you have gotten rid of them, they might even return, sometimes in a different shape or form, but with the same result. Habits have a peculiar way of working, and for some habits, that is good; for others, it is not good at all. It is all based on the simple fact that you are accustomed to doing them. You cannot change your habits by wishing to do so; you have to take action to make the change. What you will discover is that everyone around you will notice, you feel better and appreciate more what you have. This is the best start you could have to encourage yourself to take actions you never dared to take before.

GOOD HABITS
– THE HABITS SERVING YOU

When you discover your good habits, (oh yes, there are usually more than you think), you should immediately acknowledge them for their presence. Good habits are habits that serve you and make your life as good as it can be, right now. All the good habits you can find need to be appreciated, simply because they are an important part of the reasons for how you got where you are, in a positive sense. If all your habits, all your skills and your knowledge were full of negative influence, you would never read this book. You are reading this because you know that you can improve things. You can create lots of great things when you know what to do, how to do it and how to follow up. There are no limits, unless you set some.

Good habits help you keep away doubts, they also help you to work consistently and they help you to keep your belief in what you are doing. The more your habits serve you, the easier it is to create your business and your products. You will also discover that your marketing has a tendency to be quite successful, even on a more challenging day than expected. Your good habits should not be underestimated; they help you spread what is good for your clients or customers. Your websites will make you look like the person you are, and your customers want to trust you. Give them what you have, make sure they can trust you and you have the situation exactly as you want it. You are a winner, because you took the right actions inside and outside. You need them both to be good.

HOW TO CHANGE A HABIT TO SERVING YOU

The moment you discover one of your bad habits, you should start working on changing it into something that serves you. Your first task would be to define the habit, so you recognize it the moment it tries to revisit you (since you've been such close friends for such a long time). Bad habits are good at hiding, and they come crawling back in different circumstances if you don't keep an eye on them.

Your description will have an opposite, that is, a positive habit. This is what you want to change it into. When you describe this opposite, be sure to include its appearance. Its appearance will make you recognize it sooner, and it becomes easier to keep the good habit, care for it and improve it as a habit that will keep serving you for a long time.

You need to accept the old habit, to really make the change a lasting one. If you don't accept it, you will go around wondering why you used to do those "weird" things, or you could keep wondering about the reason why you should let it go. The clearer you are in your description, the sooner you will have the pleasure of saying, "thank you for letting me know, and goodbye; let's never meet again". Then, of course, you let it go. You should never give it a thought, you don't have to; bad habits always survive somewhere else. Other people learn the lesson and pass it on. No need to worry, just let it go and move on, in the direction you want to go, with your new habit. Why not celebrate it's presence?

PAY ATTENTION TO THE NEW HABITS

Learning to drive a car does require some lessons. You are not very good at it in the beginning, but you are at least good enough when you get your license. You have learned, in a habitual way, how to drive a car. Everything new has a period where it takes some time to do what we are supposed to, but as we get the hang of it, we get better, we work smarter and spend less time. New habits are no different. Your new habits need some attention, at least in the beginning.

Once you get your driver's license, all you want to do is to drive, it feels natural to do so and you feel a strong urge to drive. This is a natural way of implementing new skills and making them habitual. This is the best way of improving them, to make sure you implement them. Implementation may take some time, depending on how new they are. If it's more or less an adjustment of your previous habits, you are an expert almost immediately, but if it's totally new, you will spend more time. The more you use them, the more naturally you work. The more naturally you work, the less time you spend on the task. The moment a habit seems to be serving you and improving well, you use it as long as it serves you, but no longer.

SERVICE YOUR NEW HABITS

Regularly, you need to "refresh" your new habits. They can be hard to implement, but the more practice you get, the better they will serve you. Sometimes it's hard to remember why you should implement some of your new habits, simply because you barely use them, don't use them often enough, or worse, never use them again. The latter could be a sign of you going in the wrong direction, so pay attention to what you want and be critical of how it serves you. Sometimes we are just not ready for that specific task, but we need it. This means that you may want to buy that service until you are as good as you need to do it comfortably.

Keep in mind that everything you do should serve to improve what you do. You want to be more efficient, be nicer, work smarter and smile more often. Do not allow yourself to get stuck with a task you just can't manage YET. Keep moving around it until you are able to do it OR leave it to someone who knows what and how to do it. That is a great way of keeping you moving forward and please someone else, by letting them help you. When you always keep an eye on how you do what you do, you will learn new ways of being better and better, every day in every way. You find smarter ways of working and you find better solutions every now and again. Make sure that all your habits are serving you and change them when they don't. When you do, you will always find a new path and make your life an exciting journey.

CONSISTENT RESULTS
- HOW YOU PRODUCE THEM

What you do in the morning will have an impact on the rest of your day. To produce consistent results, preferably the results you want, you should control your mornings. When you get up, you should have a plan for the day. You make the plan the evening before, remember? Consistency is about doing what it takes consistently. If you consistently don't, then you already know the outcome. When nothing happens, nothing happens.

Even if you are working for someone else, like most people do when they start their online career, you need to have a plan for the development of your business. Always make a plan for the next day. There are of course the beneficial opportunities of making the business run itself, but you have to make a daily effort to make it work, and you have to make what you need to have it run. It doesn't happen immediately. Patience in the building of your business, not too slow, not too fast, will build your confidence and a better business. Any interruption is something you learn from.

The most important way of being consistent is to work on your business daily. The more daily effort you can afford, the better. When you work on your business daily, it's on your mind at all times, and you will get a better result. Always take notes on the next steps you need to learn, your experiences and your results (or the lack of it, believe it or not, you learn a lot from it). If you can't do your marketing because you didn't finish the material (like your product, your website or your emails) in time to publish, it is not a crisis; delays happen. You don't like it, so you try to avoid it, but it happens, especially in the beginning. On the other hand, it would be a (no, I wouldn't say) crisis, but it wouldn't help you to get the results you want, if you didn't do anything at all. Remember, you want to make your business an online success, so you can live your lifestyle.

MARKETING AUTOMATION?

One of your goals is to make a list of customers. They are interested in the products you offer and you contact them via email. When this works, you want to have your system send them emails automatically, depending on what they are interested in and even depending on how they responded to your last message. It is possible to make this work all by itself, but to get there, you need to know a lot about your customers and how to approach them in terms of what they want.

When you use your autoresponder, you send the emails to all your customers. You choose when to send it, and you can choose which customers receive your emails. When you start using an automated service, you need to know a lot more about your customers. It sounds very easy, but you can also burn a hole in your wallet here. Automation is not necessarily for beginners; it's not meant to be. It works, but you really need to know your customers to make it work.

Automation is for the marketers who have "been in the game" for some time. Companies with regular customers use it, since they have a list of customers. They know what their customers want and they keep track of what each customer does. This information tells the company what the customers' interests are. When you are new, your focus should be on making your website attractive (not necessarily in a beautiful way, but it has to stand out from the rest), you need to focus on where and how to advertise and you want to share information about your business on your business page on social media. You want as many customers as possible and by building trust, you will get the right customers. The number of people joining your business will increase as you get better and build yourself a good reputation.

Let's get back to automation; you do want it, but not before you have a regular flow of customers. Your expenses should be covered, that's a part of business. First, cover your expenses, then make a profit. Automation is of great help, but the practice and training you get by working with your autoresponder is invaluable. You learn every step in how to build your campaigns, and when you have found what works for your business, you can do more or less the same and make it go on automation. This is very powerful and you should look forward to getting there, but don't start on the wrong end. Your autoresponder will be a great help for you, you still have to write an email every now and then, but you have a setup that makes your business run easily. When people visit your website, and you have set your business right, you get a lot of customers and you know what their interests are. Your promotion pays for itself; the sales cover all your other costs and the workload is minimized. This is important to make your results consistent. The time you save should be used to keep developing your business and improving what already exists.

BUILDING YOUR LIST

If you have signed in for some help online, you left your name and your email. You are a part of a list. Everyone leaving their name and email goes on a list. I'm also a part of other people's lists. When I'm curious about what they really do, I enter my name and my email to get more information. Sometimes I buy their product, because it is good and it serves me, but I'm also an eager unsubscriber to many lists. Learning to unsubscribe is important, it's also a healthy habit and when you build your list, make sure that your customers are aware of the importance of unsubscribing.

I don't know how many emails you get, without ordering them. Many people experience the same thing; some just change their email account, while others unsubscribe. Unsubscribing is like "not wanting to enter your shop again." This is normal and a lot better than the vast numbers of people who just call it spam. I have never met anyone who likes spam, but I've met marketers who desperately send out several emails to everyone on their list, wondering why there is no response.

You have to respect your customers. To keep them on your list, you need good offers presented in a way that makes them see why they want your products. When your customers like what they see, they tell their dollars about you, and their dollars want you because you take care of them. They even invite their friends to visit your store. Never attack your customers; they are people, just like you and me. They deserve to be taken seriously. It's like entering a store and feeling welcome, if you don't, you leave, right?

Your goal is to make sure that the people on your list stay there, maybe tell some friends about the help they found on your website and help to build your reputation as the great marketer you are. Happy customers return to the stores that solve their problems. This is what gives you consistent results. It might take a while to find the right people, but when you do and you take care of them, your results will be consistent.

WHEN YOU ACHIEVE YOUR GOALS, you have this moment of magic and you see new goals

Goals are important. Without them, it doesn't really matter what you do.
Having a goal helps you to chart a course in your life and makes it easier to get there. As you constantly improve your skills and mindset, you will find there are no limits to what you can experience. Your knowledge and your insights about what works help you tremendously.

When you achieve those goals, you get the wonderful feeling of satisfaction. This feeling grows on you when you're about to make it happen and you see yourself approaching results as you wander, step by step, towards them.

You get calmer, make it happen and you feel warm inside. You also get this light in your eyes. You know what to do next based on what you did to get where you are. Now you know how to get to the new goals in a new way, even better than the last one. Your new goals brighten up your heart and you smile.

Inner peace spreads its wings inside you and you can fly. You imagine where to go next and how it will look when you get there. All you want is to get there, because...

... you won't tell, but you know. You know exactly what you want, how to get there and why, *but others don't have to know all that, not yet.* It is what drives you; it is your fuel and it will reveal itself in a way you didn't know about when you started. Surprises gives zest to life and new spice that inspires you to continue causes you to think what might work this time – just because you know where to go. You have the end, the result, in mind.

Knowing where to go doesn't mean knowing what you meet along the way. Everything can happen. Always. Everything happens, always and at the same time, but somewhere else, not known to you. It's easy to be concerned or to doubt yourself, but clearing away those limiting beliefs is something you are good at. You do it all the time, so you keep your target line clear. It's just as easy to believe things are going to be great.

Some of these actions make you react in a way that makes you feel right, and it gets right, maybe not at once, but when you do those small necessary changes or adjustments, that makes it work for you, just the way you want it to, becoming what you want it to be - You Know it is the right path to your goal. You just know it!

What you meet on your way can be temptations, frustrations, it may cause you to lose some of your power. It might even make your view foggy... You don't see the goal, you start wondering, "Is this right? Am I going in the right direction? Is this for me? is This me?..."

... and sometimes you get those steep hills, where everything is a heavy lift. It is hard to just lift a finger for what you know is right, or... is it right?

You close your eyes.

You imagine what it would be like when you reach your goals. You can see how it looks when you have finished.

You start tracking yourself on the path; you are there somewhere. You keep searching, "where am I?," and you don't give up. You go the extra mile. Slowly, you see a clearing. Slowly you open your eyes, you can see something in the fog, it gets brighter, the light begins to dissipate the fog; the light gets brighter and brighter and finally There it is, your goal!

You see your goal again, it's like having your powers refueled.

You get on top of yourself, start your engine and do your work. You see the difference between what works and what doesn't, you place your foot on your pedal and you won't stop until you're on top and you've reached your goal.

Nothing can stop you: it's like Life has made you go on automatic, everything just does what you want it to. You told yourself it would work, you kept training daily and consistently to get there and now you see the results. It does work! It Is Confirmed!

Suddenly it gets to you. You achieved your goals, you see them - the results. You can hardly believe it; you check again - you are there, at the end, your goal! You achieved your goals!

Standing there, watching the beauty of your goals, you see them. They have arrived, just in time. Your *new goals*. New directions to be chosen and staked out. And you know it,

You can do this, you know.
You have what it takes. You have done this before, just not exactly in the same way as you need to proceed now. Excitement for what you will meet on your way drives you to start the search and imagine how it will be when you get there. And you will get there. It is your new Goal.

... and then, you get the hang of it. You keep on improving your skills, your mindset, plan the goals, take them apart and make it realistic, decide a date for the finish and make sure that every detail is respectfully placed in your plan, so your goals become easier to reach. You recognize them on an entirely different level. You see more of the ways you can prevent those obstacles from trying to stop you. You become more or less unstoppable, because you know what it takes. You've been there before and you look forward to getting there again. You just love what you do.

Since you started to improve your skills, you notice everything gets easier and it's easier to get to the next level of goals.

Where will it end...

This magic moment should be for everyone – and it is.

Next best steps!

1. *Make a list of your good and bad habits. Don't panic if you find the list long. You can change all the bad ones, so imagine them on the other side of the list and see how many good habits you are about to get.*
2. *Start by solving the most obvious challenges linked with habits. You can't do it all at once. One at a time is a great way of dealing with them. You have a lot of great goals to achieve. Get used to it.*
3. *Start imagining your business, how you contact your customers, how you see the income gradually grow and become consistent. How you see your business develop, grow bigger and bigger and how you constantly learn the new skills to keep on serving your customers with new surprises.*
4. *Continue to take notes of all your ideas. Start playing with how you can combine your ideas to make your business as complete as possible, but not more than complete.*

Chapter 8

DESIGN THE LIFE YOU TRULY DESERVE

"An old man told his grandson, 'My son, there is a battle between two wolves inside us all. One is evil. It is anger, jealousy, greed, resentment, inferiority, lies and ego. The other is good. It is joy, peace, love, hope, humility, kindness, empathy and truth'. The boy thought about it and asked, 'Grandfather, which wolf wins?' The old man quietly replied, 'The one you feed.'"

- (old Cherokee anecdote)

I was sitting on my bed. The sun was shining, a very quiet day outside. My laptop on my lap, looking out the open window and sensing all the beauty outside, I was writing something. It got to me there and then. I just had to write it down, make sure the feelings and the experience of a beautiful life were expressed, that all the details were there. The details are important; they can make the difference between a good and a bad day. To savor the feeling of gratitude for experiencing this moment is worthwhile; every second of it makes me feel great. Those moments need to be treasured, so I stopped writing, just to enjoy the moment; it is now, it is here and you are reading it right now.

Imagine yourself sitting on the edge of your bed. The sun is shining, and it's very quiet outside. You have your laptop on your lap; you look out the open window, hear birds singing, sense all of the beauty outside. You are creating your marketing campaign. You study your plan, and make all the parts connect to each other. You are completely relaxed, you feel good, knowing that all the parts work. It's not your first campaign, at a time when you had to learn absolutely everything from scratch. You remember it well and appreciate everything you did. This campaign is different; you know all the details and how they work. You know where to advertise and you know a lot about the people who are interested. You are confident in the result and are grateful for all the knowledge you have, your skills, your insights. You finish it; all the parts are connected.

You start smiling, looking out the window, sensing all the beauty and feel you are a part of it. You enjoy the moment; it is now, it is right where you are now. I can see you, you're doing great, you press enter and a new part of your business is online.

REMEMBER:
YOU DON'T WANT A LIVING,
YOU WANT A LIFESTYLE

a scenario:

"Suddenly; You wake up. Panic!

The alarm clock, it didn't work!

You Rush out of bed, into the bathroom and Then...

you remember.

Those days are over.

You are not there anymore; things are different now.

You don't want to return to that time when you had nothing but worries.

Always worrying about how to get those bills paid, sitting in that cubicle, not getting the work done properly because you worry too much. Your mind drives you crazy and you want peace, but everyone is too busy to help you on track, everyone has their own worries. The fear of suddenly being unemployed...

Fetching yourself a glass of water, you look at what you made of your life during the past couple of years. Relaxing when you see what you managed to change from barely having nothing to the point where you could afford to build the house you wanted. You didn't have to choose the cheapest kitchen, but bought the one you really wanted. Looking at all the family photos from those wonderful trips all over the world. Everyone smiling at you, because you made your dream a reality.

You remember what a nightmare it was back then. Every morning, not really wanting to get out of bed, driving a couple of hours just to get to work, sitting for hours not getting things done your way, disturbed by long meetings. Making those difficult calls to solve those problems that you really didn't want. Driving for a couple of hours to get home in the evening after a long day. Exhausted, watching TV, sometimes forgetting to turn it on...

Looking back makes you wonder what made you tick...

Your vision! *You had your vision of getting away from it all, and you started your search for opportunities to get out by starting small and growing into your new future, building your house, the one you wanted for so many years, on the exact spot where you envisioned it. The wonderful view that gives you the energy to live your life as you want.*

Building your future the way you want it, from dream to reality.

This possibility was suddenly there, the opportunity you grabbed and believed in.

Helping others to make their future the way they want, and still enjoy the life you want, you made your interests become your work, and you decided when to work. You now live life on your own terms.

You go to bed; you have confirmed your dreams and look forward to working on your new goals. Those good ideas that suddenly made you see what life you can have when you go for it turned you into a winner in life, and you enjoy it.

Morning dawns, and you're smiling. You know you did the right thing by taking that first small step. Go for your ideas. Learn those skills, form good habits, get a mentor and change your world the moment you are ready. "Why didn't anyone tell me how easy it is when you have the right mindset; strange but true..."

You are used to taking responsibility for your own life now, and you constantly improve and leverage from your good habits, making you what you want, just by doing what it takes."

BEING NEW IS BEING NEW

When you are new to online marketing, there are days when everything seems hopeless. Those are the days when you have to put aside your feelings and what you had planned to do, and then do something different, serving others more than yourself.

You don't want to keep up with the Joneses anymore; you are looking for something different. It's daring, it's exciting and as you get into the habit of working for it, not hard, but smart, you catch yourself relaxing, smiling and having a good time more and more often. The more you manage to focus on your goals, the better you get to do what it takes.

Success is not about showing off in front of your neighbor; it's about doing what you like, reaching goals, setting new goals and working excitedly to reach them.

What if I run out of goals – what will I do?

It could happen, but only if you don't take yourself seriously. You need to be the leader of you and trust what you are doing. When you trust yourself, know yourself and have these new skills to get you there, ideas and goals will come to you. You create them when you work on your projects, whatever they are.

Trust them, look at them as seeds you've planted. Let them grow and harvest when you understand they are ready. Ideas and goals come to you and when you take care of them, they help you to achieve them. You don't do it for yourself alone; a lot of people are looking forward to your fulfillment of the mission and you reaching your goals.

I've never done anything successful in my life, why should I believe I can do it now?

You were successfully born, you got as far as you are in life and you know the power of YET, the little word changes everything! Hear yourself say, _"I've never done anything successful in my life, YET!"_ Can you hear the power; do you feel the drive, the urge to get started? It's like starting a car, something inside starts moving, ready to take action. Create the space needed to make your time, grab it with both hands; do what you know you can do. Start exactly where you are and build the life you want. It's not about believing, it's about knowing what you are doing. You are the creator of your life; you trust that your Infinite Intelligence is on your side, gives you the right hunches, and you listen carefully. You know that if you don't listen to your inner voice, you can be sure that someone else will grab you and make you a part of the fulfillment of their dreams, their ideas, their way, when they want you there.

You are unique and your skills are wanted. There are thousands waiting for YOUR contribution to this world. It's time to take action, and actions always love to be taken NOW! Your Fire and Your Passion grow as you understand how to take advantage of the opportunities and at a time when you are ready, as in NOW. Dollars come running to you; they see your potential and love to help you. You win, because you created a winning mindset for yourself, a winning skillset and a winning set of campaigns. Dollars enjoy that, they tell their owners to let them join your dollars and they bring many friends.

How can you say that? I don't have any skills. What could I possibly do to make the Dollars Want Me?

Everything you do is a skill. You wake up in the morning; that in itself is a call to do something other than sleep. Ask yourself:

- What else could I do, different from what I do?

- What part of what I do is something I like?

- What would I want to do if I could?

- If I had nothing at all, what would I love to do?

- If I had everything, completely free of worries, how did I get there?

When you go to bed at night, you have used tons of skills to get there. Everything you do in a day requires a skill on some level. Your likes may be a hint of what you are good at, but it doesn't mean you have to be passionate about it. Your passion is in you, somewhere. Maybe you have hidden it, because you have never had time for it. Maybe you didn't have the guts to start living that way, because everyone said you couldn't.

Many talented people are doing something other than what they are good at, because other people didn't believe in them. It is sometimes a lot easier to do what other people say, just to make sure you struggle as much as they do. When you do something you are passionate about, <u>something you "can't not do"</u>, You just Have To Do It. It doesn't feel like work. You love to do it, and it's something you love so strongly that you keep on doing it, no matter whether you get money for it or not. You just have to do it. Learning everything about it, reading, listening, watching, talking, making it, *because you can't <u>not</u> do it*. If you don't do it, if you just dream about it, well, there you go – that's the end of the story. This is solution number 1.

SOLUTION NUMBER ONE
- EVERYONE DOES THIS

You change from doing to dreaming. Then you can take it with you everywhere and no one can take it away from you. It's your precious moment, your precious talent. You want to keep it for yourself because it means so much to you. Everyone does it this way. NOW is always a good time to change that and share it with the world. People are waiting for you, and they start getting confused. What you have is what they need to make their dreams come true. They are prepared to let the dollars want you. Never stop following your Dreams, don't keep them to yourself, share them with the world, be different from everyone else. Your dreams are You.

SOLUTION NUMBER TWO
- YOU CAN'T NOT DO IT

A scenario:

"An opportunity Knocks At Your Door!

they usually don't... What to do... What to DO!

*You sit comfortably, relaxed, reading a book, listening
to music, **then**...*
You hear something;
There's a faint sound,
like someone is knocking at your door
You stop reading,
turn off the music - look towards the door;
unmistakably, there is a knock at the door.
Your heart starts beating, louder.
You didn't expect anyone, not now.
What is this...

you start walking slowly to the door,
it feels like you just have to.
You can't resist,
it's like you have no other choice!
You open the door and you see it.

It's an opportunity,

at last,

Thousands of dollars are in front of you
A complete system to gather them, too
It's an opportunity – it's HERE
At your door!
The question is,

How do you make an opportunity knock at your door?

The question is real, but you find no answer.
It found you! What to do!

You keep telling yourself,
Don't focus on the Don't !
Your **Passion** *- is your fuel.*

When you can live life for what you're
passionate about,
you will smile more,
dream more,
live more,
Give more!
You want that – a passionate life!
> *"To dream by night is to escape your life.*
> *To dream by day is to make it happen."*
> **– Stephen Richards**

You don't even think about it, you just do it!
... get to your passionate life,
Gradually see it happen,
just the way you want it.

If you could change what needs to be changed,
Would you do it?
<u>Opportunity only knocks Once.</u>

"Not knowing when the dawn will come
I open every door."
— **Emily Dickinson**

Childhood dreams normally change;

it's automatic. There are exceptions, of course, but it's normal to have another dream in your early or late teens than the one you had as a child. When you have more experience, you see more possibilities. These possibilities give rise to new goals, new ways of living. The confusion coming from all the other youngsters might rip a child's dream apart. Maybe their dream was wrong, but what if it wasn't? What did you dream of as a youngster, where would you be if you had followed that passion?

How would your life be right now?

CAREER CHANGE OR A JOB CHANGE?

There is a difference between changing careers and changing jobs. This book has to mention it, simply because success in online marketing very often ends in a career change, but not always.

As long as You know what You want, you just need to get some of the facts straight. Maybe you know already, and maybe you do not know. Start by building that confidence; get your mindset in tune and trust yourself. When you find what works for you, amazing things will happen, whether it's a job change or a career change.

WHAT IS A CAREER CHANGE?

A career change can be dramatic, but it doesn't have to be. It all starts with you wanting a change or you may be forced to change for some reason. In any of these situations, you still have the two options, changing your job or changing your career.
If you don't like what you do and want to do something else, you are looking for a career change.

This is very often mixed up with this one:
When you have a job, you do what you like, but you want to change the surroundings, work in different circumstances; if that is the case, then you are looking for another job. Still, this one is confusing, because it could also end up in another career. If you find yourself more comfortable doing what you like in a completely different type of company or want to work for yourself, you are changing your job and career.

You are definitely looking for a new job if you don't want to be the one who decides what to do, when to do it, how much you will get paid, your work hours, etc. This would not necessarily mean that you shouldn't try online marketing. Online marketing can be a secondary income, so you can still learn from these ideas on how to get started.

Doing what you like is what makes life interesting, so if you don't like what you do, you need to find what you do like. When life tells you to change something, change it. You have the resources in you, find them, let them grow strong and use them.

ONLINE MARKETING AS A CAREER CHANGE

- *Do something you like*

- *Build a reputation for yourself*

- *Build your business*

- *Take your business to another level*

WHAT STUFF ARE YOU MADE OF?

Knowing yourself is a very important aspect of running a business. When you build your business, you will meet obstacles. You need to learn a lot of new stuff that you didn't know about and this can be confusing. If you are aware of what you want, this part gets more into the habit of just doing it.

Your way of working may be the difference between failure and success, but to prevent failure, you need to know who you are and make yourself stronger. By continuing to learn what you need, by trying and testing, although you may feel like you are failing at times, you will keep moving forward, and you will be on your way to success. You just have to do what it takes for you to succeed.

Your personality has to be prepared for the changes. Sometimes it's enough just to get a grip on yourself, other times you have to go deep into your soul to achieve goals you have set for yourself and your business. No one can tell you what path you have to take, apart from you.

Who you are matters because it makes you stronger and more targeted when you gain the knowledge you need. You are preparing yourself for the next level. That's why you want to be in charge, to make sure it's your decision and not decisions made by others.

DO YOU KNOW WHAT YOU WANT TO DO?

If you are stuck on speculating about what would be the most interesting thing for you to do, you have a series of tasks ahead of you.

- *Figure out what you are passionate about. What makes you happy and what makes you feel good?*

- *Figure out how you can make money on your skills. Start with the easy ways and improve as you get more skilled. How do other people do this?*

- *Constantly improve your skills. Always be the best at what you do. Always learn something new; it widens your perspective.*

- *Find the most interesting way of marketing yourself and your passion. What feels natural is a start, what feels awkward is to be challenged.*

THE DIFFERENCE: WANT TO DO - DOING IT

If you are serious about changing jobs or your career, you likely talk about how miserable your present job is. Instead, you should be grateful for the food it gives you. If you don't have a job, but want one, you probably talk about how hard it is to get a job, and how you hate to be without one. You should be grateful for all the time you have to do what you want.

Both of these scenarios are quite common. They are based on focusing on lacking things in life. If you think like that, you are not alone. It's typical to focus on what you want by talking negatively about your present situation. To make a successful change you want your focus to be on gratitude for what you have and how much better it will be when you reach your goals.

Negative thoughts do not serve your search for the best life you can get, they misdirect your attention away from what serves you, and you easily wind up in another roundabout instead of working towards your goals. Negative thoughts are all based on fear of some kind, they are limiting beliefs. Deal with them as soon as you find them. Don't let your beliefs limit you, challenge the limits.

Make sure you:
1. Stop focusing on what's bad where you are.
2. Start taking action on what you want to do, the moment it comes to you.

Change focus:
Instead of spending all your energy on what's negative in your life, you should use it to figure out what the opposite good is. Don't let negativity run you, look at the bright side of things, where you want to be.

When you keep all that negative energy alive, you stop yourself from doing a lot of things that could make your day. You keep staying away from what you want, because you are too busy seeing a lot of negativity in the present situation.

Taking action on any idea you get is a good idea. You give yourself different experiences and maybe you will find something even more interesting than what you knew existed.

WANT TO WORK AT HOME?

There are tons of opportunities helping you to find out how you can work at home or work from home and develop your lifestyle. You have to decide, but it is better to start somewhere, rather than spending the rest of your life to decide whether you want to start. Any start is better than just talking about it. Visualize yourself into the right choice, and remember that <u>now</u> is always a good time to start.

When you start searching for opportunities or ideas online, you will be shocked by everything you can do to create a business and how to get it up and running. Everything is possible, but start by searching for the main topics of your interests and you will get the ideas that serve you best now.

Unfortunately, a lot of the opportunities online don't live up to the standard they promise. Don't believe that every solution is as good as the others are; nevertheless, they may still contain a good idea, but not always a good package.

We are all different from each other, so we are looking for different ways of creating the lifestyle we want. When someone tells you "This is the most successful business online", you may take it into consideration, but remember – this is someone else's passion. You want to attract the dollars to your passion. Examine the solutions you come across. The more research, the more you know, the better decisions you make.

BUSINESS ONLINE

What we like to do and what makes us feel good has to match to make the business a success. Working online is not just about how to make money; it is more about what you like to do. When what you do is in your interest, it is easier to keep following up and you will always see new opportunities for growing your business. The more passionate you are, the more you are willing to invest in your business. The time you invest is what makes your business grow, it is also what gives you a good reputation for taking your business seriously.

This is why most systems don't work for the majority of people. They are made to work for certain kinds of people. They usually say that the programs can be used by everyone, but frequently they are not for everyone. Many marketers make their own variant of the system, in this way they work on what they are passionate about and have found a way of making the system work according to it.

THERE ARE PLATFORMS AND THERE ARE SYSTEMS

It took me some time to figure out what I was looking for. I started in a system and wound up on a platform. If you don't know the difference between a platform and a system, here's a short explanation (and if you do know, please be patient... I thank you in advance).

- A system is made to be easy to understand, so that you don't have to learn a lot of things – you just have to take some actions.

- A platform is made to save you time on building any kind of business. You can perform any kind of activities on top of it. The time is saved by having all the coding done for you, meaning you don't have to spend months learning it. Whatever you need for your activity you will find available on a platform.

The good aspect of a system is that you reduce your activities dramatically. On the other hand, if it doesn't work for what you want to do, you can't do anything about it (unless you find a way to make it work with what you are passionate about).

The good aspect of a platform is that you can create whatever you want on top of it. You use the platform to build what you want. You have to do some work, but when you create your business; you are having fun, so you gladly do the work because you like it. If you are dissatisfied, you can change it, tweak it and make it work as you want it.

DIFFERENT PLATFORMS

Some platforms are nothing but platforms. It's usually just a website builder, with a lot of templates to choose from. They normally offer different solutions on how to build a complete business online. You get tutorials on how to build the website. In addition, you need the training to create and run your business. Few website builders offer this training, but the Internet is full of other options where you can learn what you need.

There are other platforms that have a complete business to offer in addition to being a platform. You are practically ready to earn just after you finish the training you need, to make sure you understand how it works. These platforms tend to be very expensive. The platform earns the money; you take the risk.

Many people actually stick to the business offered on the platform and are extremely successful. This means – provided you know this is right for you – that you might have to pay a lot, but you also might gain a lot. People who succeed with these platforms are usually already very skilled when they start. If you are skilled and have done a lot of online marketing, you can do it.

If you're not that skilled, wait until you are. The skills will come to you, as long as you take action and constantly learn what you need to design a good campaign and market it. When you know how it works, and have experience in making money online, you are ready for this kind of business.

Imagine that you invest in your business and when you have developed everything you want to create, you earn money at the same time. When you have finished building your system on top of the platform, you can reduce your work hours dramatically and still have a business that makes you more money than a regular job usually does.

Just for the record, a platform is mainly a website, usually with the training you need to build your business on top of it.

BUSINESS - sounds worse than it is

Small businesses run from the home are great solutions.
Having the product line at home, or having deals with
other people for the delivery are the usual ways to solve
the storage problem. Many people choose this solution to
free up more time to spend with their children, to be able
to travel more or just do what they want to do. Living
their dream, so to speak.

Those who just have a dream and don't take the
necessary action to learn how to build and run a
business, soon find that life is a nightmare.
You need to educate yourself on how businesses work.
There are public documents to sign and a few tasks
needed to be taken care of to make the business a
success. Still, this shouldn't scare you. The public
documentation is meant for your security; it is also a
confirmation on the manifestation on your dream. You
are serious, and you are in business.

Your product line needs to be taken care of as well. You
may need storage for all the items you want to sell. If you
provide some kind of service, storage facilities are not
needed, of course, but any kind of business needs
attention to run smoothly and be profitable.

THE TRAINING YOU NEED

You can find evening classes on how to get your business
up and running.

You can also find online courses. Then you are able to create your business when it suits you. By scheduling when to move on and keeping to the schedule, you will be able to do the necessary combination of developing your business and growing along with it.

Are you ready for a decision?

New Career or New Job?

DESIGN THE LIFE YOU TRULY DESERVE

Your excitement gives you a lot of energy. This energy should be kept alive by constantly reaching your partial goals. The best way to start is by describing what you have now, with a special focus on <u>what you do not want</u> to have in your life anymore. This is phase one.

> **Do This Now:** *Start writing down all the things you want to get rid of in your life; if you know why you want to get rid of it, make a note of that, too. Use the time you need for this. When you feel finished, leave some space to continue later. You will find other things as you work on the other phases of this process. It doesn't really matter how you write it down. Some people like to make stories, others make lists. The important thing is to have it in writing.*

The second phase of an optimal mapping of your future is to describe what it is you want in your life. Keep what you are satisfied with, but maybe you want more of it? Describe in as much detail as possible your new future, what you do, what you like, what you have, your surroundings, your house, your favorite color, scent, your favorite everything. There are no limits to what you can write down. You want to be this detailed so you can visualize it. Visualization is a great help for manifesting what you want. It is usually called "having the end in mind". (When do you want it?)

> **Do This Now:** *Start writing down all the things you want to have in your life, why you want to have them and what your life will be like when you have them. The more detailed, the better. Be sure to include when you want them.*

Phase three is about finding a way, drawing a "map" showing how to get rid of the things you don't want. There is no need to be concerned about how you will get to where you want. When you work on your mindset, this will come to you. You may not believe it, but keep an open mind, try to avoid the expectancy of what you know something about. Our mind works in mysterious ways, and you will be amazed when you understand the power of this great part of your body. Be prepared for taking actions you didn't know you had to take. When you change something, you will do many things differently than you are used to or that you anticipate. Just look for the opportunities, go with your intuition and you will see wonderful things happen. You will find what stops you when you make it clear what it is you don't want and why. They get even clearer when you understand what it is you want. Limiting beliefs have this strong power over us, through our habits, but using the techniques that suit you will transform them into something that serves you. We need to change those habits and replace them with the habits we want. This is usually called "be the person you want to be".

> **Do This Now:** *All the things you listed in the first phase can't be replaced at once. You need to take the time it takes. One thing at a time. Start somewhere and be aware of the ones coming. (This is why a list, a story or your favorite way of writing comes in handy)*

How will things look once you reach your goals? Visualization is the fourth step in this process. Having the end in mind is very effective for the small goals and the big ones. You will have many goals. There is one goal bigger than the rest, when all the small goals have been achieved. These goals are set when you make your changes. Every change has a goal. Some goals are to get rid of something, while others are about making or achieving something.

While reading this book, you may have gotten a sense of what your passion really is. If you haven't found your passion yet, you can simply choose a former passion from your childhood or later in life. They can be much more accessible than you imagine.

> **Do This Now:** *Imagine your life as it would be right now if you had followed your passion. You had no worries, no need for anything. Everything that matters is what you do, you feel*

good and you are living the life of your dreams.
Now: close your eyes and visualize it!
(Visualization isn't necessarily visual. Some
people have pictures; others have colors, words
or something else. You can practice on making
the visual visual; it's about trying, over and over
again. There are techniques you might want to
search for).

One last step...

NOW IS ALWAYS A GOOD TIME TO SURRENDER

This is the last step in your designing process.
Surrendering is about being grateful. When you are
grateful for what you have, you keep up the spirit to
continue what you are doing. If you always are exhausted,
you will not easily surrender. You probably don't
appreciate anything. You're too exhausted. I've been
there, but I don't allow it anymore. It's not worth it. You
shouldn't allow it either, it's not necessary and it's not
worth it.

I had this conversation with a friend of mine. He couldn't
wait to see the seaside. It was a Wednesday and he had
been working Monday until very late, got early up that
Tuesday barely able to see the end of the day, had an
early start that Wednesday, not looking forward to the
rest of the day. Another night had to be spent at work, to
prepare properly for the next day. I tried to tell him he
needed to take care of himself, but he had excuses for

everything I suggested. He was hooked into the battle of hard work. Is it true that the harder you work, the more you get paid? No, the more exhausted you get. The less happy you are, the less pleasant you are to other people. It just isn't good.

You don't have to work hard; you want to work smart. A great life is best managed when you work smart. You get more done in less time. You get more time from less work. The time you have left is for learning new things, feeling the excitement, time to be present with the people you want to be with, not people you are bound to be with. You could also just call it 'living life'.

"Every day, in every way, I'm getting better and better".

There is no end to the reasons why people drive themselves to exhaustion, most of them are not good, they also have a tendency to be driven by others, for reasons not serving them. I know a lot of people working hard like that or being told by their boss to do this to themselves. It is madness, really. It is not necessary, it's unhealthy, and it contains everything that is not good for you. You can't manage to keep track of everything; you start making mistakes, you lose sleep at night and life is, simply put, not in balance.

When your days are not working as you please, but pull you in the wrong direction, they push you away from what it is you honestly want. You are caught in someone's dream, and it can be very hard to break free from it. Your loyalty, your bills, your obligations and so forth force you into the habit of making a dream come true – not yours, but someone else's dream. You can change that.

Surrender. Look around you, accept what is, appreciate where you are. Forgive everyone for whatever they are doing to you or have done to you. Make a decision to improve your life and let life show you the way.

When you start looking for opportunities, take responsibility for yourself, trust any higher power you believe in, forgive everyone and start over, you will notice the world around you changes. The more targeted you are, the sooner and better results you get. There are no limits, unless you set them. Don't limit your challenges; challenge your limits. This sentence alone has helped me to make my platform where I will keep building my business, based on knowledge, pride, curiosity, happiness, passion and a strong wish to create a great life for me and everyone around me. It's solid ground; I know what I'm doing and it works.

Next best steps!

Read this and then make the decision. How and when do you want to start your online marketing?

Is Life something You

can Get a Grip On?

or not...

Let's say YOU CAN **GET A GRIP ON LIFE**
Would you do it?

Live the beach life?

Live the wild life?

Live life as a traveler?

Live a quiet life?

Meditate?

Live life?

We all have our dreams and wishes, they drive us through day after day, but **do** we want to live out those dreams or wishes?

Look around you,

What you see is what you have.
Is everything there, everything you want in your life?

Compare this with your biggest dream and imagine
yourself being there.

In Your Dream

What is the difference?

How can you get there, if you want...?

Or is it, if you dare...?

When we can make a dream reality, it means we can be
there – in the middle of the dream, except it is not a
dream, it's reality.

You wake up in the morning, get out of bed in your
luxury suite. When you look out the window, you see the
beach, it's sunny and the temperature is perfect for a
swim. You just have to eat some breakfast, so you order
some from room service.

What happens next is up to you...
Maybe it's just the usual: "this is never gonna happen"
Or is it the "it never crossed my mind, I can do that"?
Your dreams may be different from the above, but it's
there.

Your life is in your dream, you use it as a reason to get
through your day,
and then

You use your day as an excuse not to follow your dream...
"I will never get there, it will never happen..."

STOP

That's up to you.

Only You Can Make Your Dream Your Life

Only You

What is stopping you from being you? Did you ever think
about that?

We are very good at making excuses and continuing to do
what we have always done.

There are reasons for that, but are those reasons actually
very good?

If you should start over again, making sure your life
turned into the success you want for yourself,
how would your life be, what will it look like?

You decide what's going to happen
You did what you had to do to get where you are.
You made your life the way it is.
You believed you could make it happen.

You can make anything happen.

Your life depends on what YOU do with it.

You do this by listening to what YOU want.
It's time to start marketing yourself to yourself.

Why not start today?

... and the next postcard you send is like:

Hi, when I woke up this morning, I got out of bed in this
luxury suite.

I can see the beach from the window,
it's sunny and the temperature is perfect.

After breakfast, I will take a swim and it looks like it's
going to be such a wonderful day,
just like yesterday.

Wish you were here. Should I order a ticket for you to
come and join me?

I'll pay, I would love your company, you know that. Oops,
room service here with breakfast...

Love you

(and your signature)

www.ingramcontent.com/pod-product-compliance
Lightning Source LLC
Chambersburg PA
CBHW031808190326
41518CB00006B/239